CW00670713

IMAGES
of Sport

SWANSEA RFC

1873-1945

Aerial photograph of St Helen's ground in 1929. Shortly after this photograph was taken the pavilion buildings were demolished and rebuilt on their present site.

Swansea Rugby Club is now renowned for its pioneering end-of-season overseas tours. It was rather different on this occasion in 1938 when players and officials went on a day outing to the Gower Inn at the end of the season. The photograph includes former club president Louis Figglestone, past chairman Trevor Davies, Harry Payne, Wilf Harris and Leslie Davies.

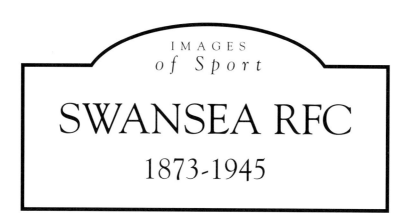

IMAGES
of Sport

SWANSEA RFC
1873-1945

Bleddyn Hopkins

TEMPUS

First published 2002

Tempus Publishing Limited
The Mill, Brimscombe Port,
Stroud, Gloucestershire, GL5 2QG

© Bleddyn Hopkins, 2002

The right of Bleddyn Hopkins to be identified as the Author
of this work has been asserted by him in accordance with the
Copyrights, Designs and Patents Act 1988.

All rights reserved. No part of this book may be reprinted
or reproduced or utilised in any form or by any electronic,
mechanical or other means, now known or hereafter invented,
including photocopying and recording, or in any information
storage or retrieval system, without the permission in writing
from the Publishers.

British Library Cataloguing in Publication Data.
A catalogue record for this book is available from the British Library.

ISBN 0 7524 2721 0

Typesetting and origination by Tempus Publishing Limited
Printed in Great Britain by Midway Colour Print, Wiltshire

Contents

Acknowledgements

The production of this book would not have been possible without the assistance of many people. The suggestion initially came from Ray Ruddick who was in the process of producing a book about Pontypool RFC and Tempus very quickly confirmed its willingness to publish. Soon my fascination was total and there was much pleasure in its compilation.

First and foremost, special thanks go to David Price and Michelle Payne for their assistance with the many items of memorabilia loaned by the club. Also to Tim Auty who made his vast private collection of photographs available at my disposal.

Thanks also to David Farmer, the *Western Mail*, Dai Richards at www.rugbyrelics.com, Simmons – Aerofilm, Ian Milne (Swansea Schools Rugby Union), Brian Simpson, Barry Griffiths, John Jenkins, Gareth Hicks, Wayne Cann, the Swansea Reference Library and the National Library of Wales, Aberystwyth.

Apologies if I have inadvertently omitted anyone from the above list of acknowledgements.

Finally my thanks go to David Price for writing the foreword to the book. He has been associated with the club for over fifty years, initially as a player, then club honorary secretary from 1955 (for thirty-seven years) and latterly as president and currently life patron.

Bleddyn Hopkins.

The 1904/05 'invincibles' squad, under the captaincy of Frank 'Genny' Gordon. The club went undefeated throughout the season, winning 28 and drawing 4 of its 32 games.

Foreword

Having enjoyed a fifty-years-plus relationship with the Swansea club in its various forms, it is with considerable pleasure I write a foreword to this most recent pictorial presentation, reflecting both the fortunes of the club and of some of its greatest players and occasions. May I also take the opportunity of referring in part to the club's distinguished history.

Swansea, 'the All Whites' was originally an association football club (1872), two seasons later (1874/75) it changed to rugby football and later (1875) it joined with the existing cricket club to become 'Swansea Cricket & Football Club'. The current title Swansea RFC Ltd dates from the age of professionalism (1995).

In March 1881 the club became one of the eleven founder clubs of the Welsh Rugby Union and its home, the world famous St Helen's ground, was formerly an international rugby venue (1882-1954) and is equally famous as a cricket centre for Glamorgan County Cricket Club.

Twenty-three Swansea players have toured with the British Lions and some 167 have played with distinction since 1882 in various Welsh National sides. Amongst this number are two of the most capped players of all time – Garin Jenkins (58 caps) and Robert Jones (54 caps).

Since its inception, Swansea has always been a leading club, both within Wales and on the international scene. Early halcyon days were in the period 1898-1914 when they were invincible (1904/05) and Welsh champions on six other occasions; they have again achieved success in the latter decades of the last century.

Notably, since the introduction of leagues (1990/91) the club has headed the Welsh premier division on four occasions, won the Challenge Cup twice (1995 and 1999) and been finalists on three other occasions. In 1995/96 Swansea reached the semi-final stage of the European Cup. The club has also recorded victories over Australia, New Zealand and South Africa in its 129-year existence.

The author and compiler (Bleddyn Hopkins) – who is incidentally a Merthyr man, but a devoted 'Jack' – is to be congratulated on his diligent research in producing the book for publication. I can commend his work both to the rugby historian and enthusiast. It will rekindle memories of some of the club's special occasions and achievements and the deeds of its multitude of players, both famous and not so famous. Comparable books have already been published on other clubs, and we are indebted to Mr Hopkins for bringing the 'All Whites' into prominence.

D.P. Price
Life Patron

The famous 'Swansea Jack' black retriever dog with its owner. The dog is reputed to have saved the lives of 27 humans and two dogs on Swansea beach. There is a monument on the promenade opposite the St Helen's grandstand today in memory of the dog's great achievements.

One
A Brief History

The club was initially formed in 1872 under association football rules and converted to rugby following a decision on 17 October 1874. It is believed the first rugby game played by Swansea was against Llandovery College on 28 November 1874. The Swansea captain on that historic day was Charlie Chambers who was to become the inaugural president of the Welsh Football Union (now WRU) in 1881. The shirt colours first adopted by Swansea were blue and white horizontal stripes. Then, for one season, the players wore a vivid scarlet. The white jersey was adopted after that, and retained. The club did not truly become 'All White' until 10 January 1925 when white shorts were worn instead of the blue ones mostly used previously.

SWANSEA

RUGBY FOOTBALL
CLUB
1873

This is a large wooden plaque on display at the club today which celebrates the formation of the Welsh Football Union (now WRU) in 1881. Swansea was among the eleven founder clubs. The Swansea club was hugely influential within the Union's formation, with three former club captains taking prominent positions. Charlie Chambers (president) and Fred Meager and A.H. Richardson were joined by H.R. Knill from the club, the last three being members of the committee. The plaque was designed and arranged by a former Swansea player Lyn Harry from Dunvant.

The highly influential Sir J.T.D. (John) Llewellyn was instrumental in saving St Helen's from prospective developers in the 1870s. He was an extremely keen cricketer and it was his passion for cricket that was decisive in his efforts to secure the ground for cricket and rugby purposes. He was later to become patron and President of Swansea Cricket and Football Club, President of the Welsh Football (Rugby) Union from 1885 to 1906 and also an MP. James Livingstone referred to him in 1900 as 'a President without precedent'.

This book entitled *The Swansea Story* was produced by Brinley E. Matthews and published in 1968. It represented the first comprehensive account of the 'All Whites' since its formation more than ninety years previously. The book contains 102 pages and some illustrations.

The club produced this comprehensive brochure containing 100 pages to celebrate its centenary season in 1973/74. The brochure includes a greeting from HRH The Prince of Wales and features by J.B.G. Thomas, Rowe Harding, Clem Thomas, Billy Bancroft and Barry John.

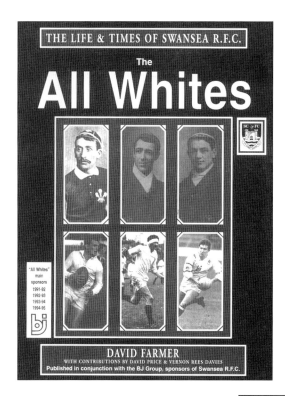

The Life and Times of Swansea RFC by David Farmer was published in 1995. It represents the most definitive history of the 'All Whites' and chronicles (in 200,000 words) the achievements of the club over 120 years with many illustrations featured.

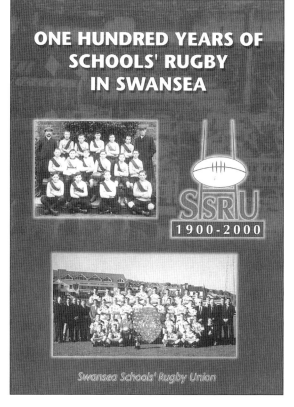

The Swansea Schools Rugby Union (SSRU) celebrated its centenary in 2000/2001 and this brochure is a dedication to the first 100 years. Some of the more famous Swansea schoolboy international players prior to the Second World War were Jack Bancroft, Bruce Barter, William Bowen (1912), Leslie Davies, Tom Day, Wilf Harris, Brinley Lewis, Edgar Long, Eddie Morgan, Bert Palmer, Dai and Tom Parker, Harry Payne, Bob Smitham and Frank Williams.

12

Two
The Developing Years

This was the medal presented to the team for winning the Challenge Cup in 1880. The names of the players depicted on the medal are as follows: from top to bottom, left-hand column: C.L. Bath, R.H. Brown, F.J. Carlyle, E. Clark, T. Clark, S. Croot, J. Doggett, D. Gwynn. Right-hand column: W.H. Gwynn, E.M. Jones, F.C. Jones, F.F. Meager, A.H. Richardson (captain), W.M. Roberts, W.H.A. Walters. Umpire: J.C. James.

This Swansea cap is dated 1880 and belonged to Tom Clark. It represents the earliest dated cap in the possession of the club. Tom made his debut for Swansea in 1875.

Sir George Lockwood Morris was a mobile forward and was selected for Wales' second international match (*v.* Ireland, 28 January 1882). He thus had the honour of being the first player from the club to be 'capped'. He represented Wales on 5 occasions between 1882 and 1884. George made his debut for Swansea in 1878 and captained the club in the 1881/82 and 1882/83 seasons.

Frank Purdon joined George Morris as Swansea players in the Wales team for the third international (*v*. England, 16 December 1882). He had actually played for Wales in their first two internationals but as a Newport player before transferring to Swansea in 1882. He had played mainly as a half-back for Newport but played as a forward for Wales in his 4 international appearances from 1881 to 1883.

This is believed to be the earliest club squad photograph. It has been dated as 1886 but given the players shown it is more likely to be from 1888. The players depicted are, from left to right, back row: A. Wolff, E.M. Jones, D. Burnie, A. Whapham, T. Russell. Third row: G. Bowen, W. Bowen, D. Williams. Second row: W. Smith, J. Samuel, H. Bevan, G. James, W. Wilcocks, T. Roberts, C. Coke, E. Thorogood, A. Lewis, S. Rice, D. Samuel, J. Meredith, W.J. Bancroft, A. Lewis. Front row: W. Williams, P. Jones, W.H. Gwynn, J. Morgan, J. Thomas, J. Davies, T. Blackmore, D. Morgan, T. Deacon, T. Williams.

D. Morgan played as a forward on 7 occasions for Wales between 1885 and 1889. In the game against Ireland on 12 March 1887, Morgan scored a try, which was the first occasion a Swansea player had scored in an international. He made his debut for Swansea in 1884.

These were medals belonging to W.H. Howell and E.S. Richards (captain), presented for winning the South Wales Challenge Cup in 1886/87. This was the fourth (and final) occasion Swansea had won the cup following on from 1877/78, 1879/80 and 1882/83. Evan Richards also captained Swansea in 1883/84 and 1887/88 as well as playing as a forward for Wales on two occasions against England in 1885 and Scotland in 1887.

William Henry Howell played as a forward on two occasions for Wales in 1888, against Scotland and Ireland. He made his debut for Swansea in 1887.

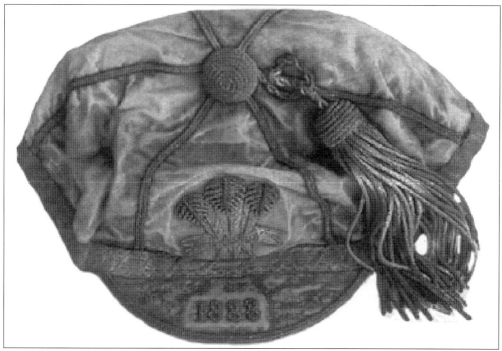

This is the cap awarded to W.H. Howell on his debut appearance for Wales *v.* Scotland on 4 February 1888. The cap is in the possession of the club and is on display in the pavilion.

George Einon Bowen played for both Swansea and Llanelli and made 4 appearances as a back for Wales between 1887 and 1888 (all as a Swansea player). George made his debut for Swansea in 1884. He also played cricket for Glamorgan and later served as mayor of Kidwelly.

John Meredith played as a forward for Wales on four occasions between 1888 and 1890. He made his debut for Swansea in 1886. He later became a literary adjudicator in Eisteddfodau and he also took a great interest in horticulture.

This image of the 1889/90 squad represents the earliest dated photograph in the club's posses-sion. Amongst the players are William Bowen (captain), W.J. Bancroft (second from right, middle row) and the James brothers, David and Evan (extreme left and right, front row).

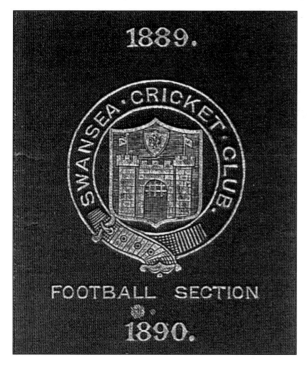

A season ticket from the 1889/90 season when Swansea were the 'premier' club in Wales. They had a playing record of played 29, won 22, drawn 3, lost 4, points for 240 and points against 56.

David (Dai) Gwynn played as a back on six occasions for Wales between 1882 and 1891. He made his debut for Swansea in 1878 and continued playing for the club until 1890. He then went to play for Oldham and captained them in 1890/91. He also played centre for the Lancashire team that won the County Championship in 1890/91. He was later associated with Swansea cricket club for many years, particularly as club umpire. He was the younger brother of W.H. Gwynn.

William Henry Gwynn played as a half-back for Wales on five occasions between 1884 and 1885 and will be remembered for being one of the first and most able advocates of the passing game. He later became the WRU's first paid secretary (1892-1896) and was also an International Rugby Football board representative (1892-1895). He made his debut for Swansea in 1880, captaining them for two seasons (1884/85 and 1885/86). He later assisted with the club's administration and served as a coach on several occasions. On 13 May 1893, he refereed the first ever soccer match between Swansea Town and Cardiff City on the Vetch field. He also played cricket for Swansea and Glamorgan. He was the elder brother of David Gwynn.

Walter Rice Evans played as a forward on three occasions for Wales between 1890 and 1891. He made his debut for Swansea in 1889. He gained a Blue at Oxford in 1890. He also played for Neath and London Welsh.

This advertisement for the Blackheath game was of special significance as it was regarded as the unofficial championship match between the 'premier' teams of England and Wales at that time. The match took place on Easter Monday, 30 March 1891 and a crowd of 18,000 crammed into the St Helen's ground to witness a magnificent Swansea victory by 1 goal, 1 try and 5 minors to 1 try.

Grand   Football   Match.

S A T U R D A Y .

KICK OFF AT 3.15.

R.N.E. College
.(DEVONPORT)
V.
S w a n s e a .

ADMISSION. SIXPENCE.   [526

Grand   Football   Match.

EASTER MONDAY.

KICK OFF AT 3-15.

B l a c k h e a t h
V.
S w a n s e a .

ADMISSION. SIXPENCE.   [5

This is a watch presented to Harry Bevan who was a forward who had made his Swansea debut in 1886. Each of the players was presented with a watch by the club president to commemorate their efforts in 1890/91 when Swansea was the premier team in Wales. The club's playing record that season was played 29, won 26, drawn 1, lost 2, points for 419 and points against 71.

The players were also awarded medals for their achievements in the 1890/91 season. This belonged to C.S. (Charlie) Coke who was a three-quarter. He had made his Swansea debut in 1890 and went on to captain the club in 1892/93.

This clock was awarded to William Arnold Bowen as the captain in 1890/91. He was a highly influential club captain for three consecutive seasons (1889/90 to 1891/92) and was reputedly liked and admired by the whole team. The impressive playing record during his three seasons in charge was played 90, won 70, drawn 9, lost 11. The team was the premier team in Wales for the first two of those seasons and runners-up in the third.

William Arnold Bowen played as a forward for Wales on 13 occasions between 1886 and 1891 and was captain against England in 1891. He was also a member of the team on 15 February 1890 that defeated England for the first time. He made his Swansea debut in 1886 and retired in April 1892 but served on the match committee for a number of years afterwards.

William J. 'Billy' Bancroft made his Swansea debut in 1889, which was the start of an extremely illustrious career. He will be remembered by most people as Swansea's greatest ever full-back. He was the club's record points scorer in 12 of the 14 seasons from 1888/89 to 1901/02. His younger brother John (Jack) also played with distinction for both Swansea and Wales for many seasons.

This photograph shows four generations of the Bancroft family outside the 'groundsman's cottage' which was situated on the south-west corner of the ground. The Bancrofts resided at the cottage until it was demolished as part of a ground redevelopment in the close season of 1891. The three standing (from left) are William Bancroft (grandfather), William Bancroft (father) and Billy Bancroft. The small boy in the front is W.J. Bancroft junior – he has been superimposed onto the main picture.

Thomas Deacon played as a forward for Wales on 4 occasions between 1891 and 1892. He made his Swansea debut in 1890 and played in the game *v.* Blackheath in 1891 for the unofficial Anglo-Welsh championship.

William Morgan McCutcheon played as a wing for Wales on 7 occasions between 1891 and 1894, having started out as a full-back for Swansea. Bill later moved to Oldham where he played with David Gwynn. He also played for Lancashire. After his playing days were over, he took up refereeing in Lancashire and was the president of Oldham Rugby League Football Club from 1924-1926.

Swansea RFC 1894/95. From left to right, back row: A.M. Jenkin, C. Coke, T. Jackson, W. Bowen (umpire). Third row : W.J. Bancroft, R.S. Jenkin, R. Messer, T. Chegwidden, E. Thorogood (captain), F. Gordon. Second row: W. Grey, S. Rice, R. Thomas, J. Williams. Front row: R. Oldham, J. Prescott, T. Blackmore.

As early as 1876 Swansea fielded two teams and by the AGM of 1880 the arrangement was formalized with the appointment of a Second XV captain. This photograph depicts the 1894/95 Seconds squad, the earliest in the club's possession.

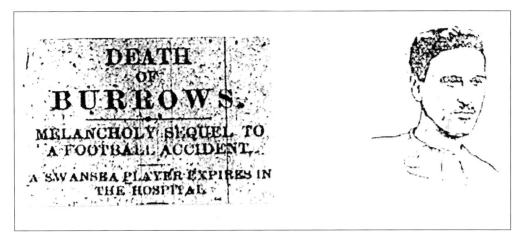

Dick Burrows had been a tenacious young player. He badly injured his neck and spine in the match against Newport at St Helen's on 23 February 1895 and was paralysed as a result. It was believed to have been a recurrence of an injury sustained some six weeks earlier. He was to die three weeks later. It is believed that this was the first occasion for a player to die as a result of a rugby accident.

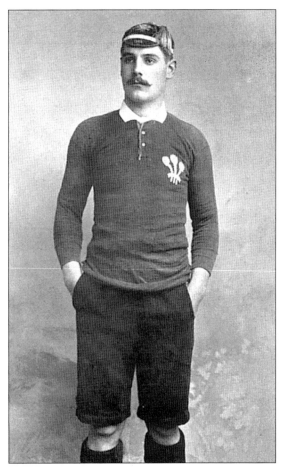

Frank Musgrave Mills was a forward who played for Wales on 13 occasions between 1892 and 1896. Frank made his Swansea debut in 1892 but left to join Cardiff for the 1894/95 season and became their vice captain in 1895/96. Frank had a 'try' disallowed in the 5 points to 4 defeat to Scotland in 1895. The goal-line had been marked by tape and the referee ruled that this tape had been stretched. It was the first time in a rugby international that one side had been beaten literally 'on the tape'.

Teddy Thorogood made his debut for Swansea in 1886. He initially played as a full-back, then retired prematurely in 1889 due to ill health. He later returned, playing as a three-quarter, and took over the captaincy for 1894/95.

Thomas Henry Jackson played as a forward on one occasion for Wales v. England in 1895. Tom made his debut for Swansea in 1893. He is believed to have been the first British international to score a try in France when he played for Swansea against 'All France' in 1899.

The James brothers (Evan left and David right) were a famous half-back pairing known as 'the Swansea gems' or 'the curly-headed marmosets'. They first played for Swansea in 1889 and represented Wales on 5 (Evan) and 4 (David) occasions, playing together 4 times. The brothers apparently played a game for Broughton Rangers in April 1892 and were offered jobs at £2 a week in Manchester. The Rugby Football Union declared them to be professional as a consequence of this. They were reinstated by the RFU upon appeal (by both the Welsh Union and Swansea) on 31 January 1896 and played until they became professional again on 28 January 1899 when Broughton Rangers signed them up (£225 down, £2 a match and a pub), taking all sixteen members of the James family.

The Brothers James

AMATEURS ONCE MORE.

REINSTATED BY THE ENGLISH RUGBY UNION.

At Leeds on Friday evening a most important meeting of the English Rugby Union Committee took place. The chief business on the agenda was to consider the question of the Brothers James, who for the past two years have been debarred from playing football owing to their attempting some time ago to transfer their services to the Broughton Rangers. The following decision was arrived at:—The com-

EVAN JAMES.

DAVID JAMES.

mittee of the English Union have decided that, on the direct application of and in deference to the wishes of the Welsh Union, the Brothers James are re-instated.

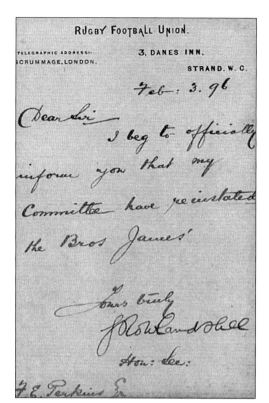

This is the RFU letter to Swansea confirming the reinstatement of the James brothers. Although the letter was dated 3 February, they were officially reinstated on 31 January and played the following day against Cardiff.

Swansea RFC 1895/96. From left to right, back row: Ted Poole (trainer), R.S. Jenkin, W. Grey, J. Williams, T. Jackson, W. Smith, Gil Evans, W. Bowen (umpire). Middle row: F. Gordon, W. Crocker, R. Oldham, A.M. Jenkin (captain), S. Rice, F. Crocker, R. Thomas, R. Messer. Front row: J. Prescott, J. Morgans.

Albert Mortimer Jenkin played as a forward for Wales on 2 occasions (Ireland 1895 and England 1896). Albert made his debut for Swansea in 1893 and was made captain in 1895/96 but resigned in the November 'because of professional duties'. Billy Bancroft took over as captain for the remainder of the season. Albert also played for Cambridge University and Glamorgan. He was ordained in 1902 and during the First World War served as an army chaplain in East Africa. He later became Archdeacon of Pretoria.

Swansea RFC 1896/97. From left to right, back row: W. Messer, W. Hill, J. Evans, Geo Davies, Hopkin Davies, S. Rice, W.J. Williams, D. Mainwaring, W. Grey, H.W. Morgan. Middle row: A. Jones, W.J. Bancroft (captain), F.J. Gordon. Front row: D. James, Dan Davies, E. James, Robert Thomas.

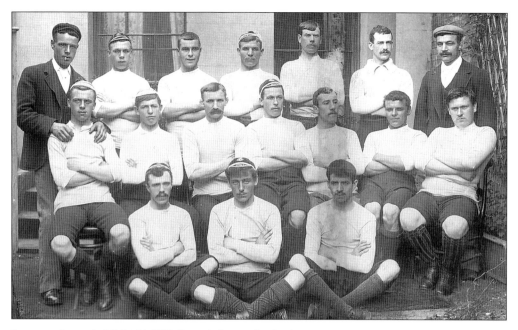

Swansea Seconds RFC 1896/97. From left to right, back row: F. Scrine, D. Thomas, R. Gibbings, J. Parker, T. Jackson, W. Davies, D. Williams. Middle row: W. Hill, A. Jones, J. Evans, Eddie Evans (captain), D. Williams (vice-captain), Dan Smith, W. Williams. Front row: H. Lloyd, H. Jenkins, D.J. Harris.

Swansea RFC 1897/98. Among the new faces in this photograph are Harry Ball, trainer, (far left, middle row) and the legendary Billy Trew (far left, front row).

Three
The Golden Era

Swansea RFC 1898/99. From left to right, back row: Harry Ball (trainer), J.L. Davies, T. Harries, G.E. Bowen, T. Jackson, W.T. Farr (treasurer), D. Harries, B. Thomas, F.E. Perkins (secretary), W. Parker, W. Bowen, J. Prescott. Middle row: D. James, F.J. Gordon, S. Rice, W.J. Bancroft (captain), A. Jones, F. Scrine, E. James. Front row: H. Davies, W.J. Trew, G. Davies, D. Rees. The 1898/99 squad were crowned Welsh club champions for the first occasion that season. Three Evans brothers represented the club that season (David, Evan and Sam). They went 'north' in January 1899, but by the end of the season the club had witnessed the emergence of two new talented half-backs, the 'dancing dicks' (Dicky Owen and Dick Jones).

UNION DES SOCIÉTÉS FRANÇAISES DES SPORTS ATHLÉTIQUES

✠NVITATION

Le Président et les Membres du Comité du **Stade Français** *prient M*.. *de leur faire l'honneur d'assister au Match international de football, qui aura lieu le Dimanche 16 Avril 1899, à 2 h. 1/2, entre l'équipe du* **Swansea Football Club** (Club Champion du pays de Galles) *et une équipe de* **Paris**.

TERRAIN DU STADE FRANÇAIS

20. Boulevard Bineau, à COURBEVOIE

MOYENS DE TRANSPORT : Gare St-Lazare ; trains pour Bécon les-Bruyères, 1 h. 50 , 2 h., 2 h. 20, 2 h. 35
Tramways : Madeleine-Courbevoie (Pont Bineau).

Les voitures sont admises sur le terrain. — Garage obligatoire pour les bicyclettes

Cette invitation rigoureusement personnelle ne pourra, dans aucun cas, donner accès sur le terrain à plus d'une personne.

De la part du Comité ....

This illustration depicts an invitation from Stade Français to Swansea to visit and play in Paris. As a result, Swansea became the first Welsh club to play in France. Due to Swansea's success during this period, the fixture was upgraded to an 'All France' team, which nevertheless, Swansea defeated easily by 30 points to 3.

The significance of this tour can be gauged by the comments of the president of the French Rugby Federation later in 1922: 'France took the game seriously as a result of the pioneer work of the Swansea team. They had always looked upon the All Whites as the greatest side playing.'

FRIDAY, April 14th.		MONDAY, April 17th
Swansea dep. .. .. 8-30 a.m.		Paris dep. .. .. 9-0 p.m.
Paddington arr. .. 1-15 p.m.		Dieppe arr. .. .. 12-55 a.m.
London Bridge Sta. dep. 9-0 ,, L. B. & S. C. RLY.		do. dep. .. immediately.
Newhaven arr. .. .. 10-40 ,,		Newhaven arr. .. .. 6-0 a.m.
do. dep. .. immediately.		do. dep. .. immediately.
Dieppe arr. .. .. 3-54 a.m.		London arr. .. .. 7-40 a.m.
do. dep. .. immediately.		do. dep. 10-45 a.m. or 3-35 p.m.
PARIS arr. .. .. 7-15 a.m.		Swansea arr. 3-55 p.m. or 8-25 p.m.

This itinerary card shows graphic details of the arduous pioneering short tour undertaken by the 'All Whites'. The journeys to and from Paris each took nearly twenty-four hours. Despite this the club and players wanted to tour again. At the club's AGM in 1900, however, James Livingstone the club chairman had to report that the Welsh Union had passed a resolution prohibiting fixtures either at home or abroad on Sundays.

This is a menu card following the game played on 16 April 1899, evidence of the French hospitality afforded to Swansea. This was the culmination of an extremely successful and popular tour.

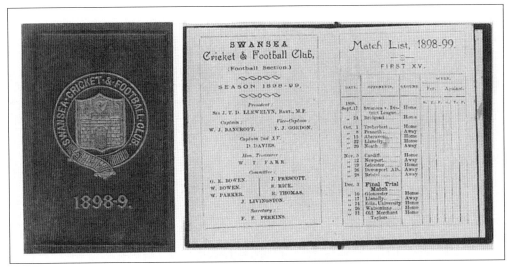

This is a season ticket from the 1898/99 season when Swansea were crowned champions. The playing record was played 35, won 29, drawn 2, lost 4, points for 732 and points against 47.

Swansea Seconds RFC 1898/99. From left to right, back row: Arthur Jones, Tom Owens, Will Jones, Aubrey Smith, M. Lee, Ernie Morgans, George Morgans (trainer). Middle row: Dai Davies, Dai Thomas, D.J. Rees, W.J. Hill (captain), Ned Jenkins, E.W. Stround, Alby Ball. Front row: Sam Howells, Dick Jones, Dick Owen, Peter Lockman.

Hopkin Davies was a forward who played on 4 occasions for Wales between 1898 and 1901. He made his debut for Swansea in 1892.

Following Swansea's visit to France the previous season, Stade Français were invited to Swansea. The game took place on 24 February 1900 and Swansea were the victors by 41 points to 0. Swansea returned the fine hospitality afforded to them the previous season in Paris by organising a banquet in honour of the French team.

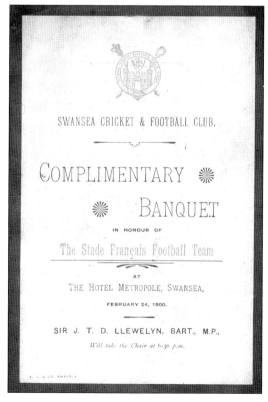

SWANSEA CRICKET & FOOTBALL CLUB.

COMPLIMENTARY ❈

❈ BANQUET

IN HONOUR OF

The Stade Français Football Team

AT

THE HOTEL METROPOLE, SWANSEA,

FEBRUARY 24, 1900.

SIR J. T. D. LLEWELYN, BART., M.P.,

Will take the Chair at 6.30 p.m.

Frederick George Scrine was a forward who played for Wales on 3 occasions between 1899 and 1901. Fred made his debut for Swansea in 1895 and was later to score the only try of the game in Swansea's unlucky defeat to New Zealand in 1905. He also played for Coventry, Cumberland and Gloucestershire.

This is Fred Scrine's final trial cap for Wales from 1900. In 1907 he received a temporary suspension by the Welsh Rugby Union for using 'improper language to a referee'. This resulted in clubmate Billy Trew refusing to play for Wales against Ireland that season in protest at the punishment.

Swansea RFC 1900/01. From left to right, back row: Harry Ball (trainer), F.E. Perkins (secretary), H. Jones, W. Parker, W. Joseph, D. Harries, J.A. Smith, F. Scrine, Sam Rice (touch judge). Middle row: R. Thomas, F.J. Gordon, Dan Rees, W.J. Bancroft (captain), George Davies, W.J. Trew, H. Davies. Front row: S. Bevan, R.M. Owen, R. Jones.

This was the first ever Barbarian team to play Swansea on Easter Monday, 9 April 1901. Swansea defeated the Barbarians team, which contained nine internationals, by 11-0, Swansea's points coming from tries by Danny Rees, 'Genny' Gordon and Fred Jowett, plus one conversion by Peter Lockman. This was the start of the traditional Easter Monday fixture, although for some of the early encounters the Swansea match took place on the Saturday and Cardiff played the Barbarians on the Monday. One of the Barbarians is quoted as saying after the game, 'I shouldn't like to play against Swansea very often, why it is harder chasing them than following the hounds, and the forwards are all as strong as blacksmiths'.

These player medals belonged to Bob Thomas and Dicky Owen and relate to the 1900/01 season. Swansea was crowned Welsh club champions for the third consecutive season in 1900/01. The playing record was played 32, won 28, drawn 2, lost 2, points for 467 and points against 81.

Robert Thomas was a forward who played on 4 occasions for Wales between 1900 and 1901, including in the three 'Triple Crown' matches of 1900. Bob made his debut for Swansea in 1892 and announced his retirement at the end of the 1900/01 season. The club wanted to honour the player who had been 'an honest Swansea scrummager for several seasons' with 'badges' to the value of £10. The Welsh Union would not sanction the presentation and the rugby writer 'Argus' in the *Cambrian* was so incensed he wrote 'The Welsh Rugby Union is not endowed with a superabundance of common sense ... its decisions are often bewildering, such as no fellah can understand'.

Billy Bancroft established a then world record 33 consecutive appearances for Wales at full back spanning the period from 1890 to 1901, captaining them on 11 occasions. He scored a total of 60 points for Wales and took every penalty awarded during his international appearances. 'Banky' also captained Swansea in 1893/94 and then for 5 consecutive seasons from 1896/97 to 1900/01 and retired after the end of the 1902/03 season.

This photograph was taken in around 1900 and depicts the old pavilion in the background. The legendary Billy Bancroft is seated second from the left. He was a very accomplished cricketing all-rounder and played as a professional for Swansea for many seasons. He made his Glamorgan debut in their first ever match in 1889 and became their first professional player in 1895. He later acted as groundsman at St Helens for many years and after retiring from county cricket in 1914 he helped coach many young players, including Gilbert Parkhouse, who went on to play Test cricket for England.

This 1901/02 cap belonged to the Welsh international D.J. Thomas who played for Swansea from 1901 up to the outbreak of the First World War and also captained the team in the 1913/14 season.

This dinner card commemorates the success of the Swansea team in being crowned Welsh club champions for the fourth successive season in 1901/02. The playing record was played 32, won 25, drawn 4, lost 3, points for 503 and points against 62. The dinner was also to commemorate the Seconds who also had a wonderful season – played 21, won 17, drawn 2, lost 2, points for 340 and points against 47.

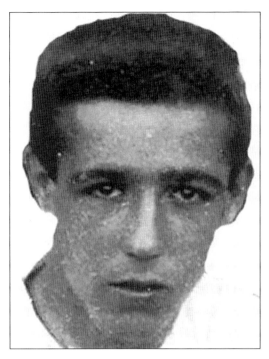

The legendary William James ('Billy') Trew first played for Swansea at Penarth on 8 October 1897 and soon established himself in the team playing in a variety of positions in the backs. He was the father-in-law of Tom Day who later played for Swansea and Wales and his son Billy Trew junior played for the club and captained them in the 1930/31 season before going 'north' to join Swinton. His brothers Harry and Bert also played for Swansea.

This Welsh Football Union medal belonged to Dicky Owen and commemorates Wales' Triple Crown in 1902. Wales defeated England 9-8, Scotland 14-5 and Ireland 15-0 and thereby secured their third Triple Crown following on from 1892/93 and 1899/1900.

William Frederick Jowett made one appearance on the wing for Wales v. England 1903. He toured New Zealand with the British Isles squad in 1904 making one appearance. He also played for Glamorgan. Fred was a prolific try-scorer for Swansea and his 42 tries in the 1902/03 season remains an all-time club record today. He played in Swansea's 'invincible' season of 1904/05 but later went 'north' to Hull KR and scored on his debut on 23 September 1905. During the First World War he served as a corporal in the Welsh ammunition column.

A.E. Freear joined Swansea in 1901/02, having taken up an appointment in the town. The wing had been capped 3 times for Ireland the previous season. He later went 'north' and joined Hull.

Swansea RFC 1902/03. From left to right, back row: D. Davies, A.E. Freear, D.J. Thomas, Sam Rice (touch judge), F.E. Perkins (secretary), J.A. Smith, E. Morgan, H. Ball. Middle row: Sid Bevan, Geo Davies (vice-captain), F.J. Gordon (captain), Dan Rees, F. Scrine, W. Joseph. Front row: W. Cole, W.J. Bancroft, R. Owen, R. Jones, W.J. Parker, W.J. Trew. The 1902/03 squad were runners-up after 4 consecutive seasons as Welsh club champions. The playing record was played 28, won 24, lost 4, points for 619 and points against 68. The Seconds also had an outstanding season in 1902/03 with a record of played 22, won 21, drawn 1, lost 0, points for 316 and points against 57.

William James Parker was a forward who played on 2 occasions for Wales against England and Scotland 1899. Will made his debut for Swansea in 1893 and captained the club in its championship season of 1903/04. He was a member of the team that played New Zealand in 1905. After he retired, he served on the committee of the club.

This was the medal presented to Peter Lockman as captain of the Second XV during 1903/04. He played as a full-back and as such spent much of the time as understudy to the legendary Billy Bancroft.

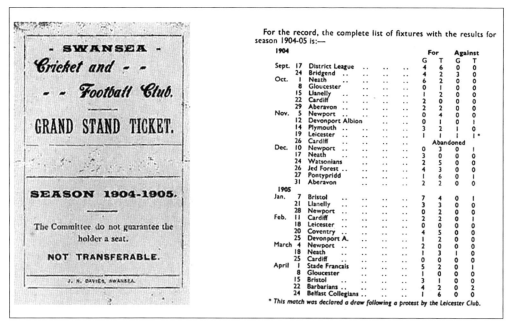

- SWANSEA -
Cricket and - -
- - Football Club.

GRAND STAND TICKET.

SEASON 1904-1905.

The Committee do not guarantee the holder a seat.

NOT TRANSFERABLE.

J. H. DAVIES, SWANSEA.

For the record, the complete list of fixtures with the results for season 1904-05 is:—

1904		For		Against	
		G	T	G	T
Sept. 17	District League	4	6	0	0
24	Bridgend	4	2	3	0
Oct. 1	Neath	6	2	0	0
8	Gloucester	0	1	0	0
15	Llanelly	1	2	0	0
22	Cardiff	2	0	0	0
29	Aberavon	2	2	0	0
Nov. 5	Newport	0	4	0	0
12	Devonport Albion	0	1	0	1
14	Plymouth	3	2	1	0
19	Leicester	1	1	1	1 *
26	Cardiff	Abandoned			
Dec. 10	Newport	0	3	0	1
17	Neath	3	0	0	0
24	Watsonians	2	5	0	0
26	Jed Forest ..	4	3	0	0
27	Pontypridd	1	6	0	1
31	Aberavon	2	2	0	0
1905					
Jan. 7	Bristol	7	4	0	1
21	Llanelly	3	3	0	0
28	Newport	0	2	0	0
Feb. 11	Cardiff	2	2	0	1
18	Leicester	0	0	0	0
20	Coventry ..	4	5	0	0
25	Devonport A.	1	2	0	0
March 4	Newport	2	0	0	0
18	Neath	1	3	1	0
25	Cardiff	0	0	0	0
April 1	Stade Francais	5	2	0	1
8	Gloucester	1	0	0	0
15	Bristol	3	1	0	0
22	Barbarians ..	4	2	0	2
24	Belfast Collegians ..	1	6	0	0

* This match was declared a draw following a protest by the Leicester Club.

This is the cover of the 1904/05 'invincible' season ticket and an analysis of the playing record in 1904/05. In 21 of the matches the opposing side had failed to score a single point. At the end of the season, Swansea stood comfortably at the top of the Anglo-Welsh table.

This is a photograph of the 1904/05 'invincible' squad. The playing record amounted to played 32, won 28, drawn 4, lost 0.

A newspaper cartoon depicting Swansea's success in 1904/05. In the last game of the season against Belfast Collegians at St Helen's, the referee stopped the game with only a minute left to play. The crowd thought the match had ended, but the stoppage was to allow both the referee and the Belfast Collegians to congratulate the Swansea team!

Frank 'Genny' Gordon made his debut for Swansea in 1894 and was later a very successful club captain for 4 seasons (1901/02, 1902/03, 1904/05 and 1905/06). During these seasons, the club was champions on 2 occasions (including the 'invincible' season) and runners-up once. He was a touch judge for Swansea's memorable win against Australia in 1908.

This illustration probably reflects how many of the opposing teams must have felt playing against Swansea at St Helen's during the club's golden era period!

These 'in memory' cards with black borders proved popular around the turn of the century. These four cards celebrate victories by Wales over England (1907) and Swansea over Newport (1903) and Cardiff (1904 and 1906).

Thomas Sidney Bevan was a forward who made one appearance for Wales v. Ireland 1904. He also toured with the British Isles team in 1904 and gained 4 caps, 3 against Australia and 1 against New Zealand. Sid made his debut for Swansea in 1897. He also played for Glamorgan. During the First World War he was commissioned as a Second Lieutenant in the 6th Battalion of the Welch Regiment.

Harry Ball had been the first team trainer for several years during the early part of the golden era. He initially retired at the end of the 1899/00 season but returned for a few more years' service.

Four

Success Against The Tourists

OFFICIAL PROGRAMME, **2d.**
A SOUVENIR.

" Y Ddraig Goch a ddyry Gychw

New Zealand
v.
Swansea

St. Helen's Field, Swansea.

Saturday, December 30, 1905.

The Maori War Song of Greeting.

Leader : It is death ! It is death !
Chorus : It is life ! It is life !
This is the strong one, the man of the brawny tribe
Who has come to us to cause the sun to shine,
Hurrah ! Hurrah !
He has caused the sun to shine !

Printed and Published by Kere Electric Press, Plymouth Street, Cardiff

Swansea hosted the final match of the tour with New Zealand having won 29 of their 30 matches, the only reverse being the infamous 3-0 defeat to Wales. Swansea lost the game by 4 points to 3 and by a drop goal to a try (Fred Scrine). Most observers felt Swansea had been very unlucky to lose the game. It is worth noting that under the modern scoring system, Swansea would have won by 5 points to 3!

FOOTBALL.

Saturday, 30th December.

NEW ZEALAND
v.
SWANSEA

KICK-OFF AT 2.45.

Admission, 1s ; Grand Stand, 2s. extra. Tickets for Seats Inside Ropes, 2s. 6d. (including admission), may be had from the Secretary

The Official Programme will be published by Mr. J. Bennett. No other publication can be sold on the ground.

F. E. PERKINS (Secretary).

THE TEAMS.

The teams were :—

Swansea.
Back :
George Davies.
Three-quarter backs :
Gordon (captain), Arnold, Ford Scale, and W. Trew.
Half - backs :
R. M. Owen and P. Hopkins.
["Rover":
S. Scrine.
Forwards :—
W. Parker, D. J. Thomas, W. Cole, H. Hunt, A. Smith, W. Joseph, and Ivor Morgan.

New Zealand.
Back :
Wallace.
Three-quarter backs :
Thompson, Deans, and M'Gregor.
Five-eighths :
Stead and Mynott.
Half - back :
Roberts.
Forwards :
Gillett (wing), Glenn, Glasgow, Gallaher, (captain), Casey, Cunningham, Corbett, and Seeling.
Referee: Mr. GM Evans.

LAST MATCH OF THE TOUR.

TO-DAY'S BIG CONTEST AT SWANSEA.

ALL WHITES AND THE ALL BLACKS.

SWANSEA V. NEW ZEALAND.

FERNLANDERS VICTORIOUS BY A POINT.

ANOTHER FORTUNATE WIN FOR THE COLONIALS.

The Swansea team on that day (30 December 1905) was: George Davies, W.J. Trew, T. Arnold, F. Gordon (captain), F. Scale, F. Scrine, R.M. Owen, P. Hopkins, Ivor Morgan, D.J. Thomas, W. Cole, H. Hunt, W. Parker, Aubrey Smith and Will Joseph.

Duncan McGregor, the New Zealand captain, considered St Helen's to have been the best ground he had played on. The tall building to the right of the picture is the site of the Cricketers hotel today.

This photograph depicts an action shot of a scrum in the game against New Zealand. Swansea had lined up with seven forwards and employed Fred Scrine as an extra back or 'rover'. The Swansea scrum appears solid and there is a hint of the New Zealand loose head prop being lifted.

This photograph depicts an action shot of a line-out in the game *v*. New Zealand. The forwards look very cluttered around the ball and somewhat disorganized. Note Swansea's forward on the right being taken out of the line-out by the New Zealand number 3.

Gil Evans played for Swansea in 1892 and later was to become a referee of some repute. He refereed the Swansea v. New Zealand game in 1905.

William Joseph played as a forward on 16 occasions for Wales in the period 1902-1906. He also appeared for Glamorgan against New Zealand in December 1905 and against South Africa in October 1906. Bill made his debut for Swansea in 1899 and played for them v. New Zealand in 1905. He was a cousin of his contemporary 'Dicky' Owen. He also played quoits for Wales in 1901/02.

Swansea RFC 1907/08. Note 'Genny' Gordon ('invincibles' captain) standing extreme left and a youthful looking Bob Dowdle (trainer) standing extreme right. The club's playing record that season was played 32, won 28, drawn 1, lost 3, points for 373 and points against 65.

Swansea Seconds RFC 1907/08. The squad is shown here captained by Fred Rees, who was later to become a club committee member.

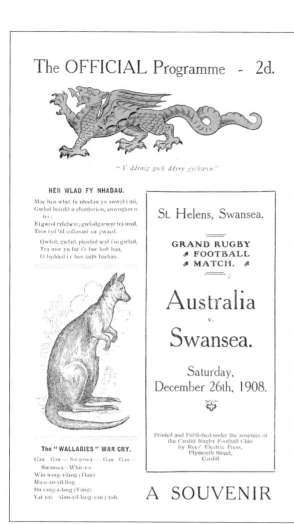

An estimated crowd of nearly 40,000 witnessed this memorable 6-0 victory over Australia, Swansea's first victory over a major touring team. Swansea's points came from an Edgar Morgan try and a Jack Bancroft penalty. The game produced gate receipts of £2,100, which at the time represented a Welsh record.

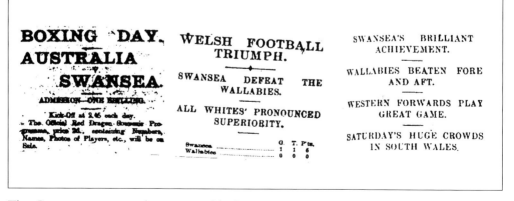

The Swansea team on that memorable Boxing Day occasion in 1908 was: J. Bancroft, W.J. Trew (captain), P. Hopkins, H. Toft, H. Thomas, R. Jones, R.M. Owen, D.J. Thomas, H. Hunt, I. Morgan, E. Morgan, G. Hayward, I. Williams, D. Griffiths, D. Davies. The 'invincible' skipper Frank 'Genny' Gordon was the Swansea touch judge that day.

Swansea RFC 1908/09. The club enjoyed a successful season as runners-up in the Welsh club championship that season, as well as defeating Australia.

The caption to this cartoon read as follows: A Rough Time. The Wallabies: Gee Whiz! This Wales is the hottest shop I've been in yet.

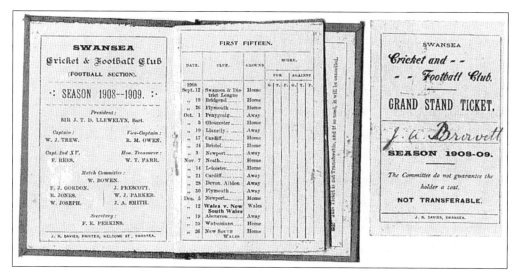

The 1908/09 season ticket. The club's playing record that season was played 33, won 27, drawn 2, lost 4, points for 368 and points against 97.

The Swansea team prepares to be transported in style from outside the Bush Hotel.

George Hayward played as a forward on 5 occasions for Wales in the period 1908/09. He made his debut for Swansea in 1905 and played in their famous victories over Australia (1908) and South Africa (1912). He later went 'north' to Wigan in December 1913, following on from two other defections earlier that season, the half-backs 'Dodger' Owen and S. Jerram.

Philip Hopkins played as a wing for Wales on 4 occasions between 1908 and 1910 and in the process scored 3 tries (1 in each of his first 3 games). Phil played in every position behind the scrum for Swansea between 1902 and 1913. He was also a member of the Swansea team that played New Zealand (1905) and Australia (1908). An athlete of great ability he also played soccer, hockey, tennis and cricket to a high standard. He rowed for his college (University College of North Wales, Bangor) at Henley and had a handicap of 4 at Pontardawe Golf Club. He was a reserve for both the Wales hockey and Wales amateur soccer teams.

F.E. Perkins acted as secretary during the club's golden era, having taken on the duties in around 1895 and remained in the role until the First World War. He was a businessman in the town and his son became club secretary in 1922.

Swansea RFC 1910/11. The team and management posed for a photograph in front of the old pavilion building.

Richard Hughes 'Dick' Jones played as a stand-off for Wales on 15 occasions in the period 1901-1910 and in the process scored 3 tries. He made his Swansea debut in 1899 and played for the next twelve years. In the process, he played his part in the club's golden era and was a member of the Swansea team that defeated Australia in 1908.

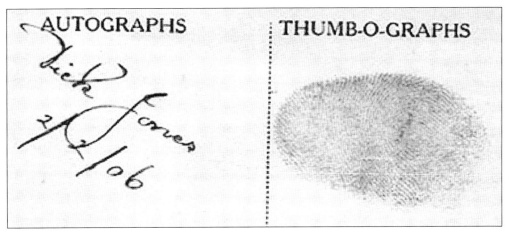

The photograph depicts Dick Jones' thumb-o-graph. For many years he formed a famous and very successful half-back partnership with 'Dicky' Owen for both Swansea and Wales. They were affectionately known as the 'dancing dicks'.

Richard Morgan 'Dicky' Owens played as a scrum-half for Wales on 35 occasions in the period 1901-1912 and in the process scored 2 tries. His games for Wales included New Zealand, Australia and South Africa as well as the traditional Five Nations countries. Although registered as Owens, he is always referred to as Owen. He was a cousin of his Swansea and Wales team-mate William Joseph. Tragically, he took his own life in 1932.

Dicky Owen's thumb-o-graph. He made his Swansea debut in 1899 and played for the next fourteen years, captaining the club in the 1911/12 season. In the process he played his part in the club's golden era and was a member of the Swansea team which played New Zealand (1905) and the team which defeated Australia in 1908.

This is 'Dicky' Owens' Wales shirt from his 35th and final international appearance. At the time this represented a British record number of caps. This occurred in 1912, *v*. Scotland when he was thirty-five years of age.

William Ivor Morgan played as a forward for Wales on 13 occasions between 1908 and 1912 and in the process scored 6 tries. Ivor made his debut for Swansea in 1905 and played for the club *v*. New Zealand (1905) and Australia (1908). His 18 tries in the 1908/09 season was a club record for a forward which stood until 1985/86. It was he who developed the loose-forward style of play by a wing-forward. He has been described as a man before his time.

Harry Hiams played as a forward for Wales on 2 occasions against Ireland and France in 1912 whilst a Swansea player. He made his debut for Swansea in 1905. He joined Llanelli in 1912/13 and scored a long-range drop goal for them against South Africa. He also played for London Welsh and Aberavon. During the First World War he served in the Royal Field Artillery.

Bertie George Hollingdale played as a forward on 2 occasions for Wales against South Africa in 1912 and England in 1913. His brother Thomas Henry played for Neath and Wales. Bert made his Swansea debut in 1912 and played for them against South Africa later that year.

Official Programme

Players' Names, No.'s, Photos and Positions.

THE SPRINGBOK

Swansea Rugby Football Club.

SOUTH AFRICANS

v.

Swansea

Thursday, December 26th, 1912

Swansea surprised everyone by gaining a famous victory over the South Africans, those 'of grand physique and exceptional speed', by one try (D.J. Thomas) to nil. This was despite playing 20 minutes of the match with only 14 men.

Swansea Rugby Football
GROUND

CHRISTMAS DAY
WATSONIANS
v.
SWANSEA.

BOXING DAY
SOUTH AFRICANS
v.
SWANSEA.

Saturday, December 28th.
NEATH v. SWANSEA.

Kick off 2.45 Each Day.

SWANSEA
v
SOUTH AFRICANS.

Official Programme, price 2d., will have coloured Springbok on front page, photos of players, names, numbers and positions.

Printers, Ross' Electric Press.

The teams were as follows:—
Swansea: Back, D. Williams; three-quarter backs, Howel Lewis, W. J. Trew, T. Williams, and F. Williams; half-backs, S. Jerram and Oswald Jenkins; forwards, D. J. Thomas, T. Morgan, D. Hollingdale, Edgar Morgan, Ben Williams, George Hayward, George Evans, and H. Moulton.
South Africans: Back, D. Morkel; three-quarter backs, R. McHardy, R. Luyt, A. Morkel, and J. Stegmann; half-backs, F. J. Dobbin and Fred Luyt; forwards, W. A. Millar, W. H. Morkel, J. Thompson, F. Knight, J. A. Francis, D. Morkel, A. Luyt, and R. H. Ledger.
Referee: Dr. J. Greenlees, of the Scottish Rugby Union.

SWANSEA'S GREAT VICTORY.

HARD-FOUGHT CONTEST AT ST. HELEN'S.

AFRICANS' LAST WELSH MATCH.

HOME PLAYER'S DAMAGED NOSE.

SPECTATORS INCENSED AT INCIDENT.

The Swansea team on that memorable Boxing Day occasion in 1912 were: D. Williams, H. Lewis, W.J. Trew (captain), T. Williams, F. Williams, S. Jerram, O. Jenkins, D.J. Thomas, T. Morgan, E. Morgan, B. Williams, B. Hollingdale, G. Hayward, H. Moulton, G. Evans.

SWANSEA CRICKET & FOOTBALL
CLUB.

South Africans v. Swansea.

COMPLIMENTARY

DINNER

IN HONOUR OF

THE SOUTH AFRICANS.

On THURSDAY, DECEMBER 26th. 1912,

AT THE

HOTEL METROPOLE, SWANSEA.

This is the card advertising the complimentary dinner arranged by the club in honour of the South African touring team.

This is a medal presented to the Swansea club by the captain of the South African team to commemorate their game in 1912.

John 'Jack' Bancroft played as a full-back on 18 occasions for Wales from 1909-1914 and scored a total of 88 points (38 conversions and 4 drop goals). He made his debut for Swansea in 1905 in a club career that spanned fifteen years, featuring as he did in the 1919/20 season. He was the club's leading points scorer for 8 consecutive seasons (1906/07-1913/14).

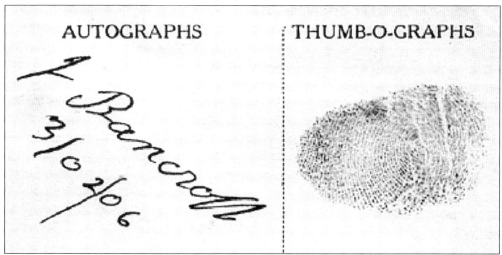

Jack Bancroft's thumb-o-graph. Jack followed his legendary brother Billy into both the Swansea and Wales teams. He also played cricket for Glamorgan from 1908 to 1922.

Billy Trew played for Wales on 29 occasions between 1900 and 1913, scoring 39 points (11 tries, 1 conversion and 1 drop goal). He played in 3 different positions, namely wing, stand-off and centre, captaining Wales in 14 matches between 1907 and 1913. He was a member of the Triple Crown sides of 1900, 1908, 1909 and 1911 as well as winning the Grand Slam in 1908, 1909 and 1911. He was a slightly built, frail figure, around 5ft 8in tall and under 11 stones in weight. He suffered numerous injuries during his career but always seemed to recover quickly, so much so that he played sixteen years for Swansea and thirteen years for Wales.

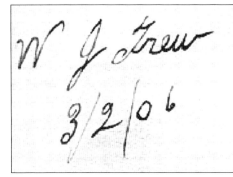

The photograph depicts Billy Trew's thumb-o-graph. Trew's illustrious career for Wales was occasionally shrouded with controversy. For instance he refused to play v. Ireland in 1907 allegedly because his club-mate Fred Scrine had been suspended by the WRU 'for using improper language to a referee'. Trew had felt the punishment was too harsh. As a consequence, the Ireland 1907 game was the first occasion there was no Swansea representative in the Wales team since the very first international on 19 February 1881.

This is the club badge from the blazer of the legendary Billy Trew from around 1910. He captained Swansea for 5 consecutive seasons from 1906/07 until 1910/11 and again in 1912/13. He played for Swansea v. New Zealand in 1905 and captained the club in their memorable victories over Australia (1908) and South Africa (1912).

Rev. Jenkin Alban Davies played as a forward on 7 occasions for Wales in 1913 and 1914 and scored 2 tries. He went on to captain Wales in 1914 but from the Llanelli club. He made his debut for Swansea in 1910. He also played for Oxford University, Cardiff, London Welsh and Glamorgan. A clergyman and schoolmaster, Alban Davies was the captain of the 'Terrible Eight' against Ireland in 1914. He served as a chaplain, attached to the Royal Field Artillery, in the First World War.

This photograph depicts the 1912/13 squad. As well as defeating the South Africans that season, Swansea were crowned Welsh club champions. Their playing record was played 37, won 29, drawn 6, lost 2, points for 457, points against 82.

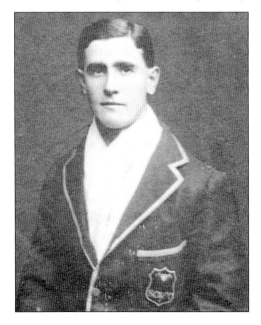

Brinley Richard Lewis played as a wing on 2 occasions for Wales versus Ireland in 1912 and 1913, scoring 2 tries. Bryn also played for Cambridge University (gaining three consecutive blues between 1909 and 1911), London Welsh and Barbarians. He was a cousin of Gwilym Michael. He was killed in action in France on 2 April 1917 during the First World War.

Edgar Morgan was a forward who played in the four internationals of 1914 for Wales. He also went on the 1908 Anglo-Welsh tour to Australia and New Zealand and gained 2 caps. He made his Swansea debut in 1907 and played in the club's famous victories against Australia (1908) and South Africa (1912). During the First World War he was commissioned as an infantry officer and later transferred to the Royal Engineers.

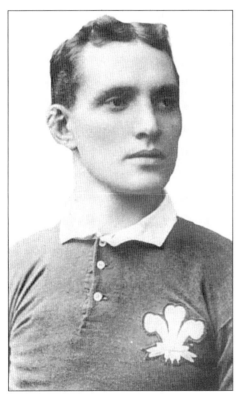

David John Thomas played as a forward for Wales on 10 occasions between 1904 and 1912. He made his Swansea debut in 1901 and continued playing for them up to the First World War, captaining the club in 1913/14. He featured in the Swansea games v. New Zealand (1905), Australia (1908) and South Africa (1912) and scored the winning try in the South Africa game. Apart from Billy Trew, he was the only player to play for Swansea in all these three games.

Swansea RFC 1913/14. This was the last full season before the outbreak of war. D.J. Thomas captained the side, a just reward for fourteen years' service to the club.

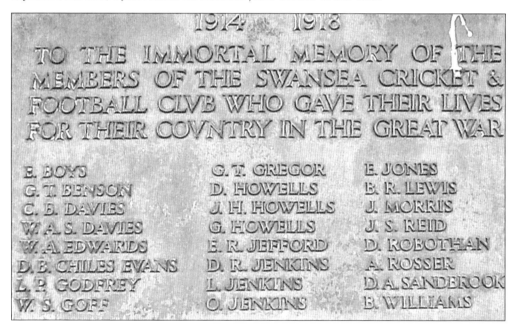

1914 — 1918
TO THE IMMORTAL MEMORY OF THE MEMBERS OF THE SWANSEA CRICKET & FOOTBALL CLUB WHO GAVE THEIR LIVES FOR THEIR COUNTRY IN THE GREAT WAR

E. BOYS	G. T. GREGOR	E. JONES
G. T. BENSON	D. HOWELLS	B. R. LEWIS
C. B. DAVIES	J. H. HOWELLS	J. MORRIS
W. A. S. DAVIES	G. HOWELLS	J. S. REID
W. A. EDWARDS	E. R. JEFFORD	D. ROBOTHAN
D. B. CHILES EVANS	D. R. JENKINS	A. ROSSER
L. P. GODFREY	L. JENKINS	D. A. SANDBROOK
W. S. GOFF	O. JENKINS	B. WILLIAMS

This is indeed a poignant reminder of the aftermath of the First World War. The plaque can be found today on the grandstand on the half-way line and lists those club members who lost their lives during the hostilities.

Five

The Aftermath
of War

Swansea RFC 1919/20. From left to right, back row: Bert Palmer, Sid Parker, Alderman W. Owen (committee), D.E. Jones (committee), A. Parker, F.E. Perkins (committee), G. Llewellyn Hay (hon. treasurer). Third row: W. Griffiths (secretary), A. Wheeler, M. Jones, F. Palmer, A.E. Jenkins, A. Evans, R. Huxtable, E. Grey, George Evans, Tom Parker, Councillor Ball (committee). Second row: R. Dowdle (trainer), D.J. John, J. Bancroft, W. Bowen, Howel Lewis (captain), Eddie Davies, Tom Morgan, Joe Rees, F.J. Gordon (committee). Front row: J. Rapsey, Trevor Davies, W. Griffiths.

Howell Lewis played as a wing for Wales on 4 occasions in 1913 and 1914. He played for Swansea from 1910 and featured in the team that defeated South Africa in 1912. He was captain of Swansea when war broke out in 1914 and captained the West Wales team that defeated the Anzacs at St Helen's on 15 April 1916. He went on to captain the club in 1919/20 before retiring on health grounds at the end of the season. During the First World War he was a captain in the Royal Welch Fusiliers.

Benjamin Beynon played as stand-off on 2 occasions for Wales against England and Scotland in 1920. The Welsh Union withheld his cap. He had never played rugby league but his 'crime' was to have accepted professional terms for Swansea Town (soccer) in 1920. Ben made his debut for Swansea in 1913 and played soccer for Swansea Town in 1914/15 after the outbreak of war. He became the first 'All White' to play rugby union (Swansea), rugby league (Oldham) and soccer (Swansea) at a senior level.

William 'Billy' Bowen played as a stand-off on 6 occasions for Wales between 1921 and 1922 and scored 2 tries. He made his Swansea debut in 1919 and joined Leeds RLFC in August 1922, scoring a try on his debut on 2 September.

Haydn Islwyn Evans played as a centre on 4 occasions for Wales in 1922, scoring 3 tries and 1 drop goal. He scored a try on his debut *v*. England and that game also featured scores by all five Swansea players – Billy Bowen, Frank Palmer and Tom Parker also scoring tries and Joe Rees claiming two conversions. Islwyn made his Swansea debut in 1920 and also played for Llanelli.

Swansea RFC 1920/21. From left to right, back row: J. John, B. Palmer, L. Jones, R. Huxtable, S. Parker, G. Evans, B. Dowdle (trainer). Middle row: F. Palmer, T. Davies, A. Evans, T. Parker (captain), J. Rees, I. Evans. Front row: T. Williams, W. Bowen, W. Griffiths.

This is a photograph of the Swansea Seconds squad 1920/21.

Swansea RFC 1921/22. Back row: A. Davies, W. Tanner, P. Evans, J.H. John, T. Parker. Third row: J. Bancroft, W. Griffiths (secretary), D.D. Evans, W. Lewis, L. Jones, J. John, G. Michael, R. Dowdle (trainer), F. Rees (committee). Second row : D. Hopkins, J.E. Evans, B. Barter, R. Huxtable (captain), I. Evans, R. Harding, F.C. Palmer. Front row: Joe Rees, T. Davies, T. Williams, R. Smitham.

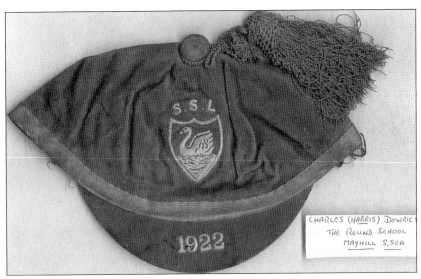

This is a Swansea schools cap from 1922. It belonged to Charles (Harris) Dowrick who attended the Round School, Mayhill, Swansea. The Swansea Schools Rugby Union has just celebrated its centenary and has been a very important part of the club's success. A number of players who won schools caps have gone on to represent Swansea and other clubs and some have aspired to full Welsh international level.

Richard 'Dick' Huxtable
played as a forward in
2 matches for Wales against
France and Ireland in 1920.
He made his Swansea debut
in 1913 and captained the
club in 1921/22.

Edwin Thomas Parker played as a
forward for Wales on 15 occasions
between 1919 and 1923 scoring 2 tries.
He also captained Wales 7 times. Tom
made his debut for Swansea in 1913 and
captained the club in 1920/21. He was
the elder brother of Dai Parker.

Rowe Harding was discarded by Llanelli but went on to play with distinction for Swansea, Cambridge University (winning 4 blues 1924-1927), London Welsh, Wales and the British Lions. He was also a top athlete winning Welsh AAA titles.

Rowe Harding and Gwilym Michael had the distinction of being chosen for the England/Wales side to meet Scotland/Ireland in the rugby centenary celebration match played on the Close at Rugby School in 1923. This was the jersey belonging to Rowe Harding from that game which England/Wales won by 21 points to 16.

Gwilym Morgan Michael played as a forward for Wales on 3 occasions in 1923 and scored 1 try. Gwilym made his debut for Swansea in 1921. He was the cousin of Brinley Lewis who also played for Swansea and Wales (2 caps *v.* Ireland in 1912 and 1913 and scored 2 tries). He served in the First World War and during the Second World War commanded a Home Guard signals detachment.

The Swansea and District rugby supporters' team, 30 April 1923. The group includes Trevor Davies (captain) and Denny Hunt (first player seated on left) who were later to serve on the match selection committees of the club. Also included are Eddie Beynon (fourth player standing, from left) Welsh international and Bryn Matthews (first non-player standing on left) later to become the club's assistant treasurer and father of Brinley, author of *The Swansea Story*.

Albert David Owen played as a stand-off for Wales *v*. England in 1924. Albert made his debut for Swansea in 1923 and later played for Cinderford. He served in the South Wales Borderers during the First World War.

Joseph Ivor Thomas Morris played as a forward for Wales on 2 occasions in 1924 *v*. England and *v*. Scotland. Ivor made his debut for Swansea in 1920 and played for the club *v*. New Zealand in 1924. He also played for Aberavon and Llanelli.

Thomas David Evans played as a centre for Wales on 1 occasion in 1924 *v*. Ireland. Tommy made his debut for Swansea in 1919 and played for the club *v*. New Zealand in 1924. He also played for Llanelli and Plymouth Albion.

Joseph Jones played as a centre for Wales on one occasion in 1924 against France. Joe made his debut for Swansea in 1923. He joined Leeds RLFC in 1924 and scored a try on his debut *v*. Huddersfield on 30 August. He won one cap for the Wales Rugby League team.

Joseph Rees played as a full-back for Wales on 12 occasions between 1920 and 1924, scoring 1 penalty goal and 2 conversions. Joe made his debut for Swansea in 1919 and captained the club in 1922/23. He was the brother of Billo Rees, the Wales and Great Britain rugby league international.

This was the jersey worn by Joe Rees against England on 19 January 1924 at St Helen's, a game in which he captained Wales. Wales lost this game by 17 points to 9 and Joe was never to play for Wales again. This is in stark contrast to his Wales debut versus England in 1920 which Wales won by 19 points to 5 and he was carried from the field in triumph by some of the 40,000 crowd.

This 1924 match represented the 17th occasion that Swansea and the Barbarians had met and the game was won by Swansea by 11 points to 9. Swansea had won the first 14 encounters, there had been a 0-0 draw in 1922 and the Barbarians secured their first victory by 23 points to nil in 1923.

Swansea RFC 1923/24. From left to right, inset: H. Jones, G. Michael, J. Jones. Back row: J. Grey, G. White, G. James, J.H. John, H. Rees, E. Thomas. Third row: E.A. Taylor (treasurer), J. Davies, I. Morris, E.C. Perkins (secretary), D. Parker, A. Parker, J. Rees. Second row: T. Harry (committee), J.E. Watkins, D.B. Jones (committee), F.C. Palmer (captain), T. Jones, T. Wilkins, F.C. Rees (committee). Front row: T. Lewis, A. Lewis.

Frank Cyril Palmer played as a wing for Wales on 3 occasions in 1922 (against England, Scotland and Ireland) and scored 1 try. Frank made his debut for Swansea in 1919 and captained the club in 1923/24. He was decorated for gallantry (MC) while serving with the 15th Battalion, the Welch Regiment, during the First World War. He was the brother of Bert Palmer who also played for Swansea and later became club secretary.

Dr D.M. Bertram, a former Watsonians forward, joined the Sketty practice of Dr Teddy Morgan the former Wales international. He joined Swansea and played for the club against New Zealand in 1924. He was capped for Scotland on 11 occasions between 1922 and 1924.

An estimated crowd of 45,000 watched the game *v.* New Zealand on 27 September 1924. The Swansea team on that day was: P. Lloyd, J.E. Watkins, T. Evans, M. Evans, D. Jenkins, Elvet Rees, R. Smitham, J.H. John (captain), Dr D.M. Bertram, G. White, Ivor Morris, Dai Parker, E. Thomas, H. Rees, Ivor Thomas.

New Zealand supporters, along with kiwi mascot, watch as Swansea are comprehensively defeated by 39 points to 3. Swansea's solitary points came from a Dai Parker penalty. Despite the score, the New Zealanders subsequently reckoned Dai Parker had been the best forward they had played against during their British tour.

George Edward Beynon played as a forward for Wales on 2 occasions in 1925 *v*. France and *v*. Ireland. Eddie made his debut for Swansea in 1923. He also played for London Welsh.

David Benjamin Evans played as a full-back on 1 occasion for Wales *v*. England in 1926. He made his debut for Swansea in 1925. He also played for Llanelli.

Swansea RFC 1925/26. From left to right, back row: W.H. Evans (secretary), E.C. Perkins (assistant secretary), W. Faull, J.H. John, W. Burgess, B. Jones, M. Rice, D. Parker, T. Hopkins, G. Grimshaw, R. Dowdle (trainer), W.R. Arnold (committee). Middle row: D.R. Jenkins, E. Hopkins, B. Barter, J.E. Watkins (captain), R. Jones, D. Hopkins, L. Shipton. Front row: S. Davies, J. Jones, E.A.H. Jones, A.L.B. Perkins.

The 1925/26 Seconds squad who managed an invincible record that season. Their playing record was played 32, won 30, drew 2, lost 0. The team was captained by Glyn Grimshaw, who later served on the management of the club and became treasurer in 1947.

Billy Trew died on 20 August 1926 and his funeral procession shown here took place on 26 August. It seemed the whole of Swansea was standing along the route from the Brooklands Hotel in Oxford Street to Danygraig cemetery to pay their last respects to the immortal man. He has been remembered as a veritable giant of the game, a player without equal. It is true to say there was only one Billy Trew!

Billy Trew junior made his debut for Swansea in September 1926 v. Cardiff, one month after the death of his father. In October he played for Swansea against the Maoris. He acted as team captain on a few occasions in 1929/30 and was elected as captain for 1930/31. At the conclusion of the season he opted to join Neath, but returned in 1932/33. A season later, however, he went 'north' and joined Swinton as a professional.

Thomas Hopkins played as a forward in all 4 home internationals in 1926 and scored 1 try. Tom made his debut for Swansea in 1925 and played for the club *v.* the Maoris (1926) and New South Wales (1927). He became one of the founders of Brecon County Rugby Union and was secretary of Ystradgynlais RFC from 1946-1970. He was the great uncle of Kevin Hopkins who also played for Swansea and Wales.

Swansea lost to the New Zealand 'Maoris' on 23 October 1926 by 11 points to 6. Danny Hopkins scored the Swansea points with 2 penalty goals. The Swansea team was : D. Hopkins, C.F. Walters, J.E. Watkins (captain), B. Barter, R. Jones, Billy Trew junior, Ivor Matthews, J.H. John, D. Parker, T. Hopkins, D.R. Jenkins, W. Faull, E. Long, P.C.M. Rice, J. Rees.

Swansea RFC 1926/27. From left to right, inset: L. Perkins, G. White. Back row: Joe Grey, Jack Rees, Roger Ling, J.H. John, D.R. Jenkins, Dai Parker. Third row: Lewis Jones (treasurer), Ben Jones, Bert Palmer (secretary), E.A.H. Jones, G. Grimshaw, M. Rice, W. Clement, Rees Evans, E. Long, Bob Dowdle (trainer), Tom Harry (committee). Second row: R.H.R. Lloyd (committee), D.P. Manley, Bruce Barter, W. Faull, J.E. Watkins (captain), D.B. Evans, D. Hopkins, W. Roberts, W.H. Evans (committee). Front row: Sid Davies, Roy Jones (vice captain), W.J. Trew junior.

Jack Elwyn Watkins was a three-quarter and captained Swansea in the 1925/26 and 1926/27 seasons. He also played for Swansea v. New Zealand in September 1924 and against the New South Wales 'Waratahs' in October 1927.

NEW SOUTH WALES

v.

SWANSEA.

1st October, 1927.

OFFICIAL SOUVENIR
PROGRAMMME : : :   **2**D.

Swansea played the New South Wales 'Waratahs' on 1 October 1927. Swansea lost the game by 11 points to 3, their score coming from a Dai Parker penalty which were the first points recorded against the tourists up to that point on the tour.

This is an invitation to the dinner given by the Mayor of Swansea in honour of the New South Wales team. The Swansea team on that day was: H.C. Perry, D.P. Manley, D.W. Evans, Bruce Barter, J.E. Watkins, Roy Jones, Sid Davies, Dai Parker (captain), J.H. John, D.R. Jenkins, Evan Harries, T. Hopkins, T. Mabbett, E. Long, W. Clement.

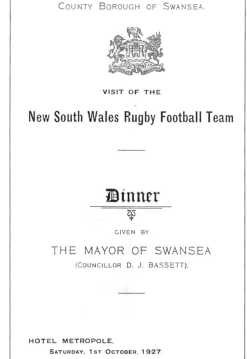

COUNTY BOROUGH OF SWANSEA.

VISIT OF THE

New South Wales Rugby Football Team

Dinner

GIVEN BY

THE MAYOR OF SWANSEA
(COUNCILLOR D. J. BASSETT).

HOTEL METROPOLE,
SATURDAY, 1ST OCTOBER, 1927.

John Howell John played as a forward for Wales on 8 occasions between 1926 and 1927. Howell made his debut for Swansea in 1921 and captained the club in 1924/25. He also played for Swansea *v*. New Zealand (1924 as captain), the Maoris (1926) and New South Wales (1927).

This photograph depicts the 1927/28 squad captained by Dai Parker.

David Stewart Parker played as a forward for Wales on 10 occasions between 1924 and 1930, scoring 1 penalty goal and 4 conversions. Dai made his debut for Swansea in 1923 and was the club's leading points scorer for 5 consecutive seasons (between 1925/26 and 1929/30). He also captained the club in 1927/28. He was the brother of Tom (Swansea and Wales) and also Alf who played for Llanelli v. South Africa in 1931.

This is a photograph of the Swansea 'Past' v. 'Present' players who took part in the D.J. Thomas memorial match 1928.

David Rees Jenkins played as a forward for Wales on 2 occasions against New South Wales 1927 and England 1929. David made his debut for Swansea in 1924 and played for the club *v.* the Maoris (1926) and New South Wales (1927). He also played for Neath. He signed for Leeds RLFC during the 1928/29 season for the sum of £370 and made his first appearance for them on 2 February 1929.

William Roy Jones played as a centre for Wales on 2 occasions against New South Wales (1927) and France (1928). Roy made his debut for Swansea in 1924 and captained the club in 1929/30. He played for Swansea *v.* the Maoris (1926) and New South Wales (1927). He served as chairman and later as president of the Swansea club.

95

Rowe Harding played as a wing for Wales on 17 occasions between 1923 and 1928 scoring 5 tries. He also toured South Africa with the British Isles in 1924 and made 14 appearances and gained 3 caps. He made his debut for Swansea in 1920 and captained the club in 1928/29, a season in which the team were runners-up in the Welsh club championship. He became a County Court judge in 1945 and a Circuit Court judge in 1953. He served as vice-president of the WRU from 1953-1956. He was also chairman and president of Glamorgan cricket club.

This photograph depicts the 1928/29 squad in Auch, France relaxing in casual dress. The squad had travelled to France at the end of the 1928/29 season for a short tour.

The photograph illustrates the team that played against Tarbes on 8 May 1929. Swansea won the game 19-13.

This is another fine example of French cuisine and hospitality. This follows the tradition set when Swansea undertook their inaugural tour to France in 1899. The menu depicts Rowe Harding's name, who was renowned for enjoying such occasions.

A SPECIMEN OF FRENCH HOSPITALITY

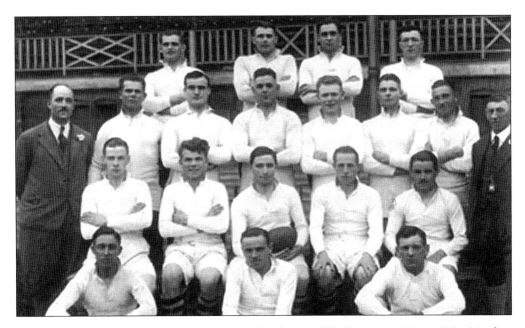

Swansea RFC 1928/29. From left to right, back row: W. Davies, J. Rees, D.P. Manley, W. Clement. Third row: R.S. Palmer (secretary), D. Thomas, Watcyn Thomas, T.L. Evans, T. Day, M. Bowen, J.E. Watkins, B. Dowdle (trainer). Second row: E. Jones, C. Davey, R. Harding (captain), Roy John, Denver Rees. Front row: W.J. Trew junior, T.A. Hill, W. Thomas. The team were runners-up in the Welsh club championship in 1928/29 with a playing record of played 42, won 29, drew 3, lost 10, points for 554 and points against 267.

This is a series of caricatures depicting the Water Rats cricket team. The team comprised present and past Swansea rugby players. The team played from shortly after the First World War up until the late 1980s.

Aerial photograph of St Helen's ground 1929. St Helen's got its name from a sixteenth century convent of Augustinian nuns, which was dedicated to St Helen. The convent had been situated in close proximity to the playing fields. St Helen's hosted the first home Wales rugby international against England in December 1882. It remained an international venue until 1954.

Swansea RFC 1929/30. From left to right, back row: R. Dowdle, D.B. Jones, Lewis Jones, G. Davies, J. Rees, C. Davey, T.A. Hill, D.F. Thomas, T.B. Day, E. Jones, J.H. John, D. Thomas, Councillor W. Owen, R.S. Palmer, Bruce Barter. Middle row: J.P. Tyler, Ben Jones, J. Evans, W. Davies, D.P. Manley, Roy Jones (captain), E. Howell Jones, E. Long, D. Parker, W. Griffiths. Front row: W.J. Trew junior, Idwal Rees, Bryn Evans. The team were runners-up in the Welsh club championship in 1929/30 with a playing record of played 41, won 30, drew 3, lost 8, points for 589 and points against 215.

William Guy Morgan played as a centre for Wales on 8 occasions between 1927 and 1930 scoring 3 tries and 1 drop goal. He also captained Wales on 4 occasions. He made his debut for Swansea in 1926. He also played for Cambridge University (winning four blues between 1926 and 1929), Guy's Hospital, London Welsh and the Barbarians. He made 45 appearances for Glamorgan Cricket Club. He was the nephew of Welsh internationals Edward 'Teddy' Morgan and William Llewellyn Morgan.

Watcyn Gwyn Thomas played as a forward for Wales on 14 occasions between 1927 and 1933 scoring 2 tries. He captained Wales in their first victory at Twickenham in 1933 and in the 2 remaining games that season. He made his debut for Swansea in 1928. He also played for Llanelli, Waterloo, London Welsh, Barbarians and Lancashire. He was later to become chairman of the English Schools RU selectors and coached the Under-19 team. He was selected as captain for the first ever Welsh Secondary Schools team in 1923.

This is the 1930 Lions (to New Zealand and Australia) jersey that belonged to Dai Parker. The Lions jersey was blue in colour then and not the red that it is today. On tour, Dai played a total of 15 games in New Zealand (gaining 4 caps and scoring a penalty in the first international) and the 1 game in Australia, against the national XV.

This was the jersey belonging to Dai Parker and is from the 1930 England/Wales v. Scotland/Ireland commemorative match played at Twickenham.

This photograph depicts the 1930/31 squad in front of the stand. The team that season was captained by W.J. Trew junior.

William Davies, known as 'Sgili', played as a forward for Wales on 4 occasions between 1931 and 1932 scoring 1 try. He made his debut for Swansea in 1928. He initially played as a scrum-half and centre before moving into the forwards. He played for Swansea against South Africa in 1931. His son Billy later played at forward for Swansea.

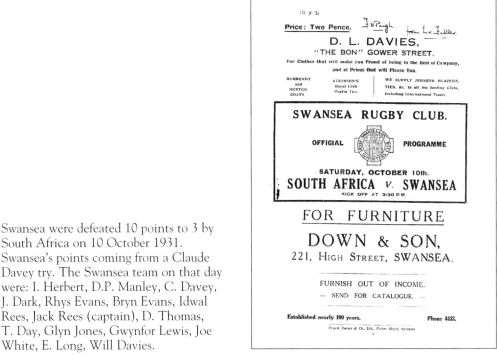

Swansea were defeated 10 points to 3 by South Africa on 10 October 1931. Swansea's points coming from a Claude Davey try. The Swansea team on that day were: I. Herbert, D.P. Manley, C. Davey, J. Dark, Rhys Evans, Bryn Evans, Idwal Rees, Jack Rees (captain), D. Thomas, T. Day, Glyn Jones, Gwynfor Lewis, Joe White, E. Long, Will Davies.

The caption that accompanied this newspaper cartoon was Dame Wales (introducing the visitors): 'Here we have Swansea, the only people with a geranium in the window. Swansea have not lost an inter-club game this season.'

This action photograph from the Swansea *v.* South Africa game shows Will Davies kicking the ball out of play, having been surrounded by South African players.

This action photograph from the Swansea *v.* South Africa game shows Eddie Long kicking the ball away when tackled by the opposition.

Swansea RFC 1931/32. From left to right, back row: J.W. Faull, Ernest Davies J.P., Lewis Jones MP, R.S. Palmer (secretary), L. Evans, Dennis Hunt, J. Gwilliam, D. Edgar Thomas, Glyn Davies, Gwynfor Lewis, Edgar Long, T.A. Hill, Clifford Cowling, M. Bowen, Trevor Davies, Tom Harry, Bruce Barter. Middle row: Tom Day, W. Davies, C. Davies, I. Davies, Idwal Rees, Jack Rees (captain), Bryn Evans, L.V. Michael, I. Herbert, Glyn Jones, Joe White, R.W. Dowdle (trainer). Front row: Dudley Folland, D. Emlyn Davies. The team were runners-up in the Welsh club championship in 1931/32 with a playing record of played 39, won 26, drew 5, lost 8, points for 400 and points against 208.

This is an action photograph from the game v. Blackheath in October 1934 at St Helen's, which Swansea won by 10 points to 8. It was the first occasion the teams had met since 1891 when the two clubs were involved in a bitter dispute regarding the share of the 'gate' receipts.

Thomas Brynmor Day played as a forward for Wales on 13 occasions between 1931 and 1935. He made his debut for Swansea in 1928 and played for the club against South Africa in 1931. He also captained Swansea in 1933/34. He was the son-in-law of W.J. 'Billy' Trew.

David John Thomas played as a forward for Wales on 11 occasions between 1930 and 1935. He made his debut for Swansea in 1929 and played for the club against South Africa in 1931. He also captained Swansea in 1934/35.

Six

New Zealand 1935 ...
History in the Making

3.30. P.m. THE MIGHTY
ALL BLACKS.

4.45. P.m. THE MIGHTY
ALL WHITES.

JACK JONES
35.

This is a cartoon depicting the captains' reactions before and after the game, following Swansea's famous victory by 11 points to 3.

SWANSEA 11   NEW ZEALAND 3

NEW ZEALAND v. **SWANSEA**

ST. HELEN'S GROUND   ::   SWANSEA

:: SATURDAY, SEPTEMBER 28th, 1935 ::

KICK OFF
3-30 P.M.

SWANSEA RUGBY CLUB

OFFICIAL PROGRAMME

Price - TWO PENCE.

Published by THE SWANSEA & DISTRICT RUGBY SUPPORTERS CLUB.
Tel. No.: 82054.   Hon. Secretary: FRANK JOHNS, 46, WALTERS ROAD, SWANSEA.
Ernest Davies & Co., Ltd., Fisher Street Printing Works, Swansea.

Section F   Row L   No. 27

ST. HELEN'S GROUND   ::   SWANSEA
Saturday, September 28th, 1935.
Kick Off 3-30 p.m. sharp

New Zealand
v.
Swansea

Stand Ticket   NUMBERED AND RESERVED
(INCLUDING TAX)   **5/-**

THIS portion of Ticket must be given
up, but the Counterfoil kept by the
Bearer as a Voucher for Seat.

R. S. Palmer,
Secretary.

ONLY ENTRANCE:
BACK OF GRAND STAND.

Swansea's win resulted in them becoming the first club side to defeat the Southern Hemisphere 'big 3', following victories over Australia (1908) and South Africa (1912). Swansea had also gained the distinction of being the first club side ever to defeat a full New Zealand touring team. Their 11 points coming from Claude Davey (2 tries), Dennis Hunt (try) and a Wilf Harris conversion. Wales followed this success by beating New Zealand by 13 points to 12 in a thrilling game on 21 December 1935. Five Swansea players represented Wales that day – Claude Davey, Idwal Rees, Haydn Tanner, Harry Payne and Don Tarr.

THE MATCH OF THE SEASON
AT ST. HELEN'S

NEW ZEALAND
v. **SWANSEA**

GRAND STAND TICKETS **5/-**   INSIDE the ROPE TICKETS **3/-**
Numbered and Reserved   Numbered but Not Reserved
CAN BE OBTAINED FROM R. E. PALMER, 4, MELBOURNE PLACE, SWANSEA.
ADMISSION: FIELD 1/-; ENCLOSURE 2/6   KICK-OFF 3.30 p.m.
BOYS 6d.   —   GATES OPEN 1 o'clock.

Swansea v. All Blacks
The ONLY OFFICIAL SOUVENIR PROGRAMME is issued by the
Swansea Rugby Supporters' Club. PRICE 2d.

ALL BLACKS WELL BEATEN

Brilliant First-Half Tries Do The Trick

HISTORIC TRIUMPH

Tanner, Davies and Davey
Outstanding

HISTORY MADE AT ST. HELEN'S

1905 and 1924 Defeats Avenged

HOW THE TEAMS FIELDED

SWANSEA :
Full-back :
EDRYD JONES.
Threequarters :
GRANVILLE DAVIES, CLAUDE DAVEY, RON WILLIAMS, G. GRIFFITHS.
Half-backs :
HAYDN TANNER,   W. T. H. DAVIES.
Forwards :
E. LONG,   W. E. HARRIES,   D. WHITE,
JOE WHITE,   D. HUNT,
H. PAYNE,   D. J. TARR,   G. H. TAYLOR.

0

Forwards :
G. T. ADKINS,   A. LAMBOURNE,   C. PEPPER,
J. G. WYNYARD, R. R. KING, W. R. COLLINS, J. E. MANCHESTER (capt.).
H. F. McLEAN,
Half-back :
M. M. CORNER,
Five-Eighths :
T. H. C. CAUGHEY ;   E. W. TINDILL.
Threequarters :
N. A. MITCHELL,   G. GILBERT,   M. J. BALL.
Full-back :
D. SOLOMON.
NEW ZEALAND :

Referee : Mr. F. G. Phillips, Pontardulais.

NEW ZEALANDERS CONQUERED BY A BETTER TEAM

ALL WHITES RISE TO GREAT HEIGHTS OF BRILLIANCE

DAZZLING HALF-BACKS

BY PENDRAGON
SWANSEA   (11pts.   NEW ZEALAND   3pts.)

DINNER TO THE NEW ZEALAND AND SWANSEA PLAYERS

TOURISTS SATISFIED WITH THE RESULT OF THE EPIC BATTLE

AFTER the great Rugby match at St. Helen's, on Saturday, between Swansea and New Zealand, players and officials of both clubs were the guests of the Mayor (Ald. W. J. Davies) at the Hotel Metropole.

Jack Manchester, the New Zealand captain, proclaimed, 'tell them back home we were beaten by all means, but please, not by a couple of school kids', referring of course to the Gowerton grammar 'schoolboy' half-backs Haydn Tanner and Willie Davies.

Edgar Cecil Long played as a forward for Wales on 7 occasions between 1936 and 1939. Edgar made his debut for Swansea in 1925 and played for the club against the Maoris (1926), New South Wales (1927) and South Africa (1931). He also captained Swansea in 1935/36, including their memorable win *v.* New Zealand.

The Swansea and New Zealand players line up facing each other prior to the kick-off.

Dennis Hunt scores Swansea's first of three tries against New Zealand. Note the photograph was reproduced on the headed paper of Dennis Hunt and Co., his own turf accountants business.

This photograph shows the Swansea and New Zealand forwards grappling for line-out possession. The four Swansea players in the line-out are (from left to right) Dennis Hunt, George
Taylor, Harry Payne and Donald Tarr.

Willie Davies looks to attack New Zealand with his 'schoolboy' compatriot and cousin Haydn
Tanner in close support.

This is a photograph of the Swansea team that was successful against the 'All Blacks', together with club officials. Note Bob Dowdle by this time had completed 30 seasons as first-team trainer and had presided over the 1904/05 'invincible' season, the narrow loss to the 1905 'All Blacks', and the wins against Australia (1908) and South Africa (1912). Swansea continued with their policy of bringing back exiled players (Edryd Jones and Claude Davey) for the 'big' games.

This is a wooden crest commemorating Swansea's historic 11-3 victory against New Zealand on 28 September 1935. It was made and donated to the club by a Mr Martin, a local carpenter. Each of the victorious team was presented with a blazer and the crest design was used for the badge on these blazers.

Donald James Tarr played as a forward for Wales on one occasion against New Zealand in 1935, but broke his neck in this game. Don made his debut for Swansea in 1933 and played for the club in their memorable win *v.* New Zealand in 1935. He also played for Cardiff, Royal Navy, Barbarians and Hampshire.

113

The Swansea and District Rugby Supporters Club officials and committee from the 1935/36 season.

Swansea players and officials *c.* 1935/36 about to board a train. The Swansea players include Eddie Long, Harry Payne, Jim Lang, Willie Davies, Gwyn Griffiths and Wilf Harris.

Seven

The War
Looms Large

Claude Davey is pictured here (right)
alongside his Wales team-mate Wilfred
Wooller. Davey played as a centre for
Wales on 23 occasions between 1930
and 1938 scoring 5 tries. He also
captained them on 8 occasions. A
ferocious tackler, he made his debut for
Swansea in 1928 and played for the club
against South Africa (1931, scoring a
try) and New Zealand (1935). He also
played for Sale, London Welsh, who he
captained between 1945 and 1947,
Rosslyn Park, Barbarians, Lancashire
and Berkshire. He later became
president of Cwmgors RFC.

James Lang played as a forward for Wales on 12 occasions between 1931 and 1937, scoring 1 try. He is best remembered for his domination of the lineout in the game against the 1935 All Blacks, which ensured victory for the Welsh team. Jim made his debut for Swansea in 1936, having joined from Llanelli.

John Idwal Rees played as a centre/wing for Wales on 14 occasions between 1934 and 1938, scoring 1 try. Idwal made his debut for Swansea in 1928 and played for the club v. South Africa in 1931. He also played for Cambridge University (winning blues in 1931 and 1932), London Welsh, Edinburgh Wanderers and Barbarians.

Ronnie Williams made his Swansea debut in 1931 and played for the club v. New Zealand 1935, partnering Claude Davey in the centre. He also captained the club in 1936/37.

Harry Payne played as a forward for Wales on one occasion against New Zealand in 1935. He made his debut for Swansea in 1931 and played for the club v. New Zealand in 1935. He also captained the club in 1937/38. He served with the Royal Marines during the Second World War and played in two service internationals.

The Swansea schools rugby team had an invincible season in 1937/38, including winning the Dewar Shield. Their playing record was played 12, won 12, points for 236 and points against 18. The photograph shows team and officials with the shield. From left to right, back row: W.G. Williams, A.G. Fuge, J.M. Williams, J.S. Jones, A.B. Jones, H.J. Griffiths, E.J. Matthews, L.G. Francis. Third row: Ivor Evans, P.T. Millard, J. Harwood, E. Harris, D. Wales, H. Mainwaring, W. Richards, W. Ambrose. Second row: B.C. George, H. Jenkins, A. Jenkins, W. Henley, F. King, W. Fisher, M. Halden, J. Ahearne, L. Quick, H. Jones, E.H. Evans. Front row: W.W. Ward, A.J. Mayne, J. Shefford, N. Rogers, E. Jenkins, Ken Thomas (captain), G. Scrines, W. Jones, Trevor Davies, Harry Davies. Sitting: A. Davies, E. Riley.

Wilfred Jones, hooker of the Swansea boys XV, tackles a Cardiff player in the final of the Dewar Shield at The Gnoll, Neath.

The Swansea schoolboys, in jubilant mood after the final whistle, carry aloft their captain Ken Thomas. Swansea beat Cardiff in the final by 16 points to 3.

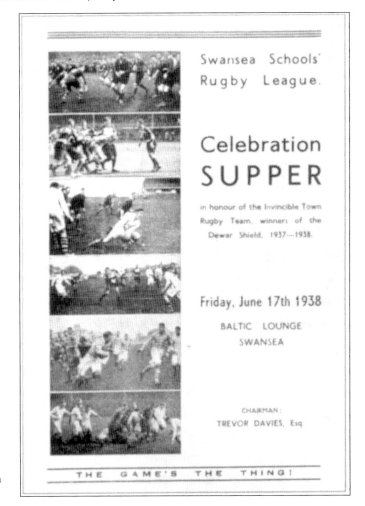

Swansea Schools' Rugby League.

Celebration
SUPPER

in honour of the Invincible Town Rugby Team, winners of the Dewar Shield, 1937—1938.

Friday, June 17th 1938

BALTIC LOUNGE
SWANSEA

CHAIRMAN:
TREVOR DAVIES, Esq

THE GAME'S THE THING!

The Swansea Schools' Rugby League arranged a celebration dinner in honour of the achievements of the Swansea team in the 1937/38 season.

These are the seven Swansea players who had toured with British teams in the period up to 1939. They are from left to right, top row: Sidney Bevan (1904), Fred Jowett (1904), Edgar Morgan (1908). Bottom: Rowe Harding (1924), Dai Parker (1930), Eddie Morgan (1938) and Haydn Tanner (1938).

William Thomas Harcourt Davies played as a centre/stand-off for Wales on 6 occasions between 1936 and 1939. In 1939, he scored the last drop-goal, valued at 4 points, for Wales in their final international before the outbreak of war. Willie made his debut for Swansea in 1934 and played for the club v. New Zealand in 1935, as one half of the famous 'schoolboy' half-backs. He also played for Headingley and London Welsh. He joined Bradford Northern RLFC in August 1939 for £1,000 and represented both Wales (9 caps) and Great Britain at rugby league. He appeared in five rugby league cup finals and was a winner in three of them. He won the Lance Todd trophy for the man of the match in the 1947 final. He is a cousin of his famous half-back partner Haydn Tanner.

This is a squad photograph relating to the 1938/39 season, captained by Wilf Harris.

Wilf Harris made his debut for Swansea in 1931 and played for the club *v*. New Zealand in 1935. He also captained the club in 1938/39.

Leslie Davies (better known as 'Bychan') played as a forward for Wales on 2 occasions against Scotland and Ireland 1939. He made his debut for Swansea in 1934 and played for the club v. New Zealand in 1935. He later served on the club committee. In his early days he had played for Bonymaen with some success.

Bob Dowdle had been the first-team trainer since 1903 up until 1939. He had also been trainer for the Seconds for 5 years prior to that as well. He had presided over much of the club's success during the 'golden era' and was trainer for the club's three memorable victories over Australia (1908), South Africa (1912) and New Zealand (1935). He had been a competitive long distance walker prior to his long association with the club.

1939-40.

Swansea Cricket & Football Club

Football Fixture List.

Committee.

Messrs. Coun. William Owen (*Chairman*).
Bruce Barter.
Trevor Davies.
Louis Fligelstone.
Bryn Matthews.

Captain 1st XV.: E. Morgan.

SWANSEA 1st XV. FIXTURES.
SEASON 1939-40.

Date	CLUB	Ground	For (G)	(T)	(P)	Against (G)	(T)	(P)
1939								
Sept. 9	Bristol	H						
" 16	Aberavon	A						
" 23	Cardiff	A						
" 30	Neath	H						
Oct. 7	Llanelly	H						
" 12	Neath	A						
" 14	Richmond	A						
" 21	Cardiff	H						
" 28	Blackheath	A						
Nov. 4	Cross Keys	H						
" 11	Llanelly	A						
" 18	Cardiff	A						
" 23	Neath	H						
Dec. 2	Old Cranleighans	H						
" 9	Newport	H						
" 14	Cambridge U.	H						
" 16	Australians	H						
" 25	Watsonians	H						
" 26	University A.U.	H						
" 30	Leicester	A						
1940								
Jan. 6	Penarth	A						
" 13	Newport	A						
" 27	London Welsh	H						

First Fifteen Fixtures—Continued.

Date	CLUB	Ground	For (G)	(T)	(P)	Against (G)	(T)	(P)
1940								
Feb. 10	Llanelly	H						
" 17	Leicester	H						
" 24	Bristol	A						
Mar. 2	Aberavon	H						
" 13	Bridgend	A						
" 16	Pontypool	H						
" 23	Harlequins	H						
" 25	Barbarians	H						
" 30	Aberavon	A						
Apr. 4	Penarth	H						
" 6	Neath	A						
" 13	Llanelly	A						
" 18	Aberavon	H						
" 20	Cardiff	H						
" 22	Cross Keys	A						
" 27	Pontypool	A						

This ticket does not entitle admission to the Club match versus Australia on December 16th, 1939, nor to the Final Welsh Trial Match which will be held at Swansea, on January 6th, 1940.

This was the season ticket issued in 1939/40. With the declaration of war, conscription and with no means of honouring the terms of their lease, Swansea Cricket & Football Club surrendered its tenure of St Helen's field to the Borough Council. In effect, Swansea RFC had ceased to exist!

Morgan Edward Morgan played as a forward for Wales on 4 occasions between 1938 and 1939. He played for the British Isles on their 1938 tour to South Africa, playing on 14 occasions and gaining 2 caps. Eddie made his debut for Swansea in 1937 and was club captain in 1939/40. He also played for the Barbarians.

Christmas Howard Davies played as a full-back for Wales on 6 occasions between 1939 and 1947, thus being one of the few internationals to have played either side of the Second World War. He played in two Service and two Red Cross internationals. Howard made his debut for Swansea in 1937. His two pre-war internationals were as a Swansea player whereas his four post-war internationals were as a Llanelli player.

Haydn Tanner played as a scrum-half for Wales on 25 occasions, spanning a career of fourteen years between 1935 and 1949. He captained Wales on 12 occasions and also captained the Barbarians against Australia in 1948. He played for the British Isles on their 1938 tour to South Africa, playing on 10 occasions and gaining 1 cap. He made his debut for Swansea in 1934 and played for the club v. New Zealand in 1935, as one half of the famous 'schoolboy' half-backs. He also played for Cardiff (captaining the side between 1947 and 1949), London Welsh, Bristol and the Barbarians. During the Second World War he appeared in 8 Service and 4 Victory internationals. He is a cousin of his famous half-back partner Willie Davies.

Eight

Bridging the Gap

This chapter is intended to provide some continuity and linkages between the period of this book (up to 1945) and the next volume, which will cover the period 1945-2003. Above: Swansea First XV Captains 1919-1968. From left to right, back row: Roy Sutton, Mike Thomas, Morrie Evans, John Leleu, W.O. 'Billy' Williams, Dil Johnson. Third row: Dai Thomas, Bryn Evans, John Faull, Gordon Morris, Rees Williams, Gwyn Lewis, Len Blyth. Second row: D.J. Davies, Harry Payne, Eddie Morgan, Dewi Bebb, R.C.C. Thomas, Tom Day, W.J. Trew junior, Ronnie Williams. Front row: Howell Lewis, J. Elwyn Watkins, Roy Jones, J.H. John, Judge Rowe Harding, Clive Rowlands, Dick Huxtable, Bryn Evans, Jack Rees.

During the Second World War, rugby at St Helen's was kept alive thanks to the sterling efforts of a small band of enthusiasts, who also had the war effort at heart and assisted charities with the takings from especially arranged matches. The photograph relates to a game that would have been played during the Second World War. The team contains a number of Swansea players (Haydn Tanner is captain), and depicts a South Wales XV who, during the war, played the RAF, British Army, New Zealand RAF and AA Command.

Bruce Barter made his debut for Swansea in 1921 and played for about 10 seasons. He played for Swansea *v.* the Maoris in 1926 and the New South Wales Waratahs in 1927. He was a Wales reserve on several occasions. After his retirement as a player, he joined the club committee and became chairman of selectors. He chaired the steering committee which organized the centenary year (1973/74) celebrations and also served as club president. He died in 1978. His brother-in-law was the former Swansea player Roy Jones. Bruce was also a Glamorgan county tennis player.

Acknowledgements
David Price's Swansea XV (1873-1945)

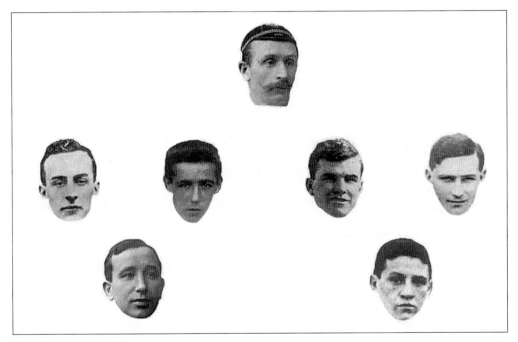

It is virtually impossible for me to nominate a 'Best' pre-Second World War XV, primarily as I saw some but not all of the listed names play. The selection is therefore based partly on reputation, partly on international appearances and partly on what I have read and on local hearsay. Backs (as illustrated): Full-back: Billy Bancroft. Three-quarters: Idwal Rees, Billy Trew, Claude Davey, Rowe Harding. Half-backs: Dick Jones and Dicky Owen. Billy Trew is my nomination as captain of this team.

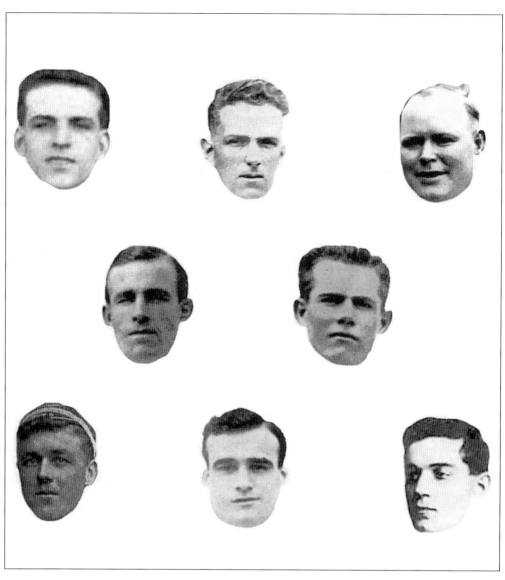

Forwards (as illustrated): Front row (top): Dai Parker, J. Howell John, Tom Day. Second row (middle): Tom Parker, Dai Thomas. Back row (bottom): Ivor Morgan, Watcyn Thomas, Bill Joseph. Perhaps not surprisingly all fifteen players were full Welsh internationals.

D.P. Price (Life Patron).